NATIONAL GEOGRAPHIC

OUR WORLD

STUDENT'S BOOK **5**

SERIES EDITORS
JoAnn (Jodi) Crandall
Joan Kang Shin

AUTHOR
Ronald Scro

NATIONAL GEOGRAPHIC

L E A R N I N G

Australia • Brazil • Mexico • Singapore • United Kingdom • United States

NATIONAL GEOGRAPHIC OUR WORLD

Let's sing! TR: B41

This is our world.
Everybody's got a song to sing.
Each boy and girl.
This is our world!

I say 'our', you say 'world'.
Our!
World!
Our!
World!

I say 'boy', you say 'girl'.
Boy!
Girl!
Boy!
Girl!

I say everybody move ...
I say everybody stop ...
Everybody stop!

This is our world.
Everybody's got a song to sing.
Each boy and girl.
This is our world!

Unit 1 Extreme Weather 4

Unit 2 Copycat Animals 20

Unit 3 Music in Our World 36

Units 1-3 Review 52

Let's **Talk**   It's my turn 54

               Who's going to make notes? 55

Unit 4 Life Out There 56

Unit 5 Arts Lost and Found 72

Unit 6 Amazing Plants! 88

Units 4-6 Review 104

Let's **Talk**   Can I borrow your bike, please? 106

               It could work 107

Unit 7 Volcanoes 108

Unit 8 Reduce, Reuse, Recycle 124

Unit 9 Wonderful Holidays! 140

Units 7-9 Review 156

Let's **Talk**   Definitely not! 158

               Our presentation is about … 159

Irregular Verbs 160

Cutouts 161

Stickers

Extreme Weather

In this unit, I will ...
- talk about types of extreme weather.
- describe the damage storms can cause.
- identify ways to prepare for extreme weather.
- write a personal narrative.

Tick T for *True* or F for *False*.

1. The temperature is freezing cold.　T　F

2. This person is walking carefully on the ice.　T　F

3. There was a hurricane.　T　F

4. The trees are covered with ice.　T　F

Versoix, Switzerland

5

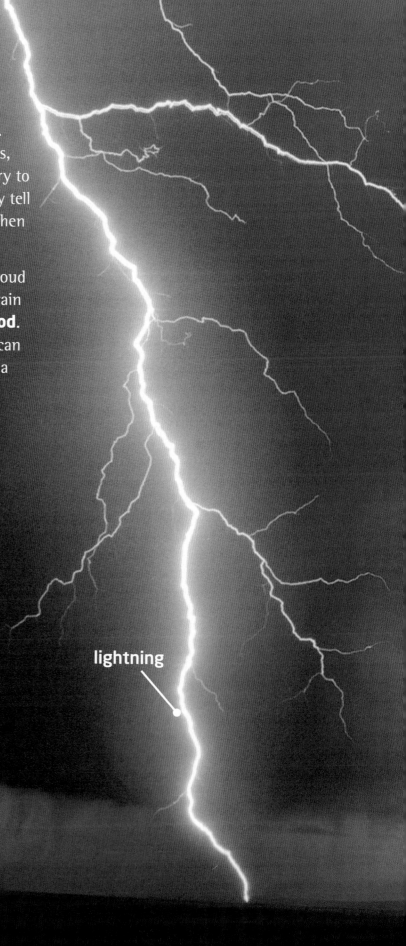

1 **Listen and read.** TR: A2

2 **Listen and repeat.** TR: A3

We know we can't control the weather. It can be beautiful, wild and dangerous, often all at the same time. Scientists try to predict weather in different ways. They tell us when extreme weather is coming. Then we can try to protect ourselves.

Thunderstorms bring heavy rain with loud **thunder** and **lightning**. If too much rain falls in a short time, it can cause a **flood**. Too little rain makes the land dry and can cause a **drought**. When it's very cold, a rainstorm can turn into a **hailstorm** or a **blizzard**.

lightning

a hurricane

a sandstorm

Wind is a dangerous force. In a **tropical storm**, the wind **speed** can be more than 100 kilometres (60 miles) per hour. Wind in a **hurricane**, or cyclone, is even faster.

A **tornado** is a column of wind that spins very fast. High winds in dry places such as deserts can pick up sand and cause a **sandstorm**.

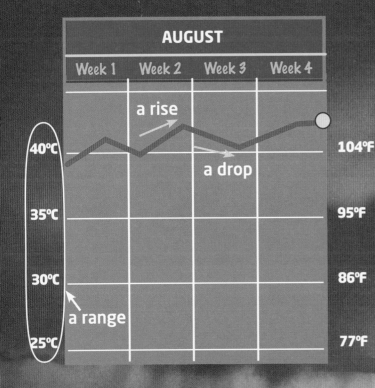

AUGUST			
Week 1	Week 2	Week 3	Week 4

a rise

a drop

40°C .... 104°F

35°C .... 95°F

30°C .... 86°F

a range

25°C .... 77°F

We can only live within a specific **range** of temperatures. At times, temperatures **rise** too high or **drop** too low. It not only feels bad, it can be dangerous! In a **heatwave**, the weather stays very hot for days or even weeks.

3 **Work with a friend.** What did you learn? Ask and answer.

It's been above 35°C all week. Is that a heatwave?

Yes, it is! Let's go swimming.

7

4 **Listen, read and sing.** TR: A4

Bad Weather

There's bad weather on the way!
There's bad weather on the way!

Is it going to rain? Yes, it is!
Is there going to be a storm? Yes, there is!
Is there going to be thunder and lightning? Yes, there is!

There's going to be a storm. I'm going to go inside!

Be prepared for emergencies.
It's always good to be safe, you'll see.
Get supplies and a torch, too.
Seek shelter. It's a safe thing to do!

Is there going to be a blizzard? Yes, there is!
Is there going to be a hailstorm? Yes, there is!
Is it going to be cold? Oh, yes it is!

There's going to be a blizzard. I'm going to go inside!

Be prepared for emergencies.
It's always good to be safe, you'll see!
Get supplies and a torch, too.
Seek shelter. It's a safe thing to do!

Is there going to be a hurricane? Yes, there is!
Is the wind going to howl? Yes, it is!
Are the waves going to rage? Yes, they are!

There's going to be a hurricane. Let's evacuate!

Be prepared for emergencies.
It's always good to be safe, you'll see.
Get supplies and a torch, too.
Seek shelter. It's a safe thing to do!
Seek shelter. It's a safe thing to do!

5 **Work with a friend.** Ask and answer.

1. Do you remember a bad storm in your town?
2. What did you do to prepare?
3. What did you think and feel during the storm?

GRAMMAR TR: A5

Is it **going to** rain tomorrow? No, it's **going to** snow tomorrow.
I'm **going to** listen to the weather forecast at eight o'clock.
He's **going to** put on his snow boots.

6 **Write.** What is the weather going to be like?

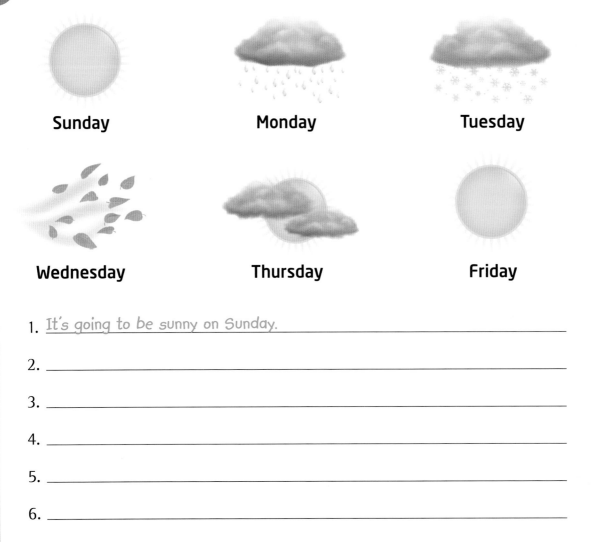

Sunday   Monday   Tuesday

Wednesday   Thursday   Friday

1. It's going to be sunny on Sunday. _____

2. _____

3. _____

4. _____

5. _____

6. _____

7 **Work with a friend.** Read. Ask and answer. Take turns.

1. Why can't we go to the park tomorrow? (rain)

2. Will she get wet walking in the rain? (take an umbrella)

3. Why is she closing the windows? (rain)

4. When will he get a new raincoat? (today)

8 **Write.** What are you going to do? Write sentences.

A thunderstorm is coming. _____

_____

_____

_____

A heatwave is coming. _____

_____

_____

_____

A hurricane is coming. _____

_____

_____

_____

9 **Work with a friend.** What about you? Talk about today and tomorrow.
Ask and answer.

A blizzard is coming.

That's right. It's going to snow a lot. Let's play inside.

10 **Listen and repeat.** Then, read and write. TR: A6

an emergency

a plan

a torch

supplies

evacuate

a shelter

When a weather forecaster predicts bad weather, you can make a

_____plan_____ to prepare. To protect yourself from wind and

rain, you should go to a _____. If the electricity goes

off, use a _____ to see in the dark. You can store

_____ in a safe place so that you have food to eat.

A really bad storm can affect the whole town. In an _____

like that, people have to _____ and go where it is safer.

11 **Listen and stick.** Find out what to do next. Place your stickers in the
correct order. Work with a friend.
Summarise the weather forecast. TR: A7

> A hurricane is coming.
> It's an emergency.

> Yes, I put emergency in
> number 1. That's correct.

1   2   3   4   5

If the weather **is** cold, I **put** my winter coat **on**.
If I **see** lightning, I **go** inside.
If a sandstorm **comes**, I **close** all the windows.

12 **Match and make logical sentences.** Then, write five sentences of your own in your notebook.

I see lightning when I'm swimming	I look for a boat.
it rains	I wear gloves and boots.
a storm comes	I try to stay cool.
the temperature rises	I get out of the water.
a flood comes	I go inside the house.
it snows	I take an umbrella.

13 **Play a game.** Cut out the cards on page 161. Play with a friend. Take turns. Match and make sentences. Keep the cards.

If it rains, I take an umbrella.

Tornado Trouble

Tornadoes happen all over the world. There is even a place called Tornado Alley. Josh Wurman studies extreme weather. He joined a team of other scientists to study tornadoes in Tornado Alley. One day, the blue sky turned black. A giant cloud came towards the team. The cloud had winds that moved in a circle. Inside his van, Wurman watched the storm through his window and on his instruments. Colours on the computer screen showed where the rain fell and where the wind was strongest.

The winds twisted the storm tighter and tighter into the shape of a funnel. When the funnel touched the ground, it became a tornado! The tornado looked like a giant grey elephant's trunk. It moved one way, then the other way. As the tornado moved across the ground, the team moved dangerously close. They dropped special instruments close to the storm. These instruments showed wind speed, temperature and how much rain was falling.

The tornado twisted and moved for half an hour. The team watched the storm and their instruments the whole time. Then the tornado leant over slowly like a soft rope. Poof! It was gone. The excitement was over. But Wurman and his team have a lot more work to do. The information from their instruments will help them to predict other tornadoes so that they can warn people and save lives.

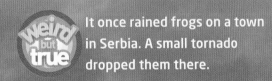

Weird but true

It once rained frogs on a town in Serbia. A small tornado dropped them there.

15 **Work in groups of three.** Discuss and answer the questions.

1. What shape is a tornado?
2. Where does a funnel touch to become a tornado?
3. Why do scientists study tornadoes?
4. What do scientists use to learn about tornadoes?

16 **Work with a friend.** How does a tornado form? Match the text to each step. Discuss.

a. Warm and cold air currents twist winds into a funnel. Then the funnel touches the ground.

b. Warm air and cold air come together. They make a twisting wind of air that moves in circles.

c. The twisting air stands up. Warm air moves up. Cold air moves down.

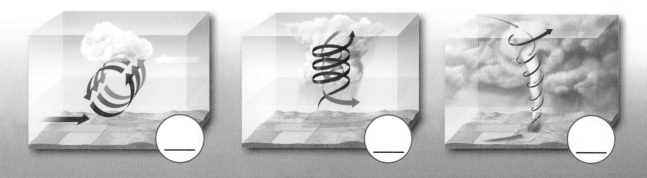

17 **Work in a group.** Compare tornadoes and hurricanes. Discuss. Complete the table.

Tornado	Hurricane
	Origin: They form over water.
	Duration: They last a week.

Personal Narrative

A personal narrative tells a story. It describes something that happened. A good writer describes details using the senses – sight, sound, taste, smell and touch. Readers should feel like they were really there. You can use words like *after*, *before*, *next* and *then* to show the sequence of events.

18 **Read.** Read the personal narrative. How does the writer describe the hurricane? How does the writer describe what she hears and sees? How does she feel? Circle the words that relate to the senses and emotions. Underline the words and expressions that show the sequence of events.

Safe, not sorry!

Last year, the weather forecaster told us that a hurricane was coming. A hurricane is always scary, but quite exciting, too. When a hurricane comes, we know what to do. We have a family plan. First, I had to help my dad put heavy wood over the windows. It was hard work.

When the hurricane came, we could hear the strong winds outside. We could hear the heavy rain coming down. Then, suddenly, we heard a really loud noise. And then something hit our house really hard! Everyone was worried. What was that noise? After the storm, we walked outside. We could see part of a tree on our roof! I was so happy that the windows were all fine. Next time, I won't say the wood is too heavy.

19 **Write.** Write about an extreme weather experience. Give details using the senses. Help the reader feel what you felt.

20 **Work in a small group.** Share your writing.

NATIONAL GEOGRAPHIC
Mission

Understand weather.

- Why is it important to understand weather? Work in a group. Discuss.

- How can you learn more about extreme weather?

- What do you do in dangerous weather? Write your ideas in the box.

'It all started when I was about six years old and saw that fantastic tornado in The Wizard of Oz.'

Tim Samaras
Severe Storm Researcher
Emerging Explorer

We make a plan.

_____

_____

_____

_____

- Share your ideas with another group. Are they the same or different? Decide which ideas everyone thinks are best.

Storm chasers, Oklahoma, USA

21 **Find out how windy it is.**

1. Work in small groups to make a wind-speed indicator.

2. Make an X with two pieces of cardboard. Staple it.

3. Staple one paper, or plastic, cup to each of the four ends.

4. Colour one of the cups with a felt-tip pen.

5. Push a drawing pin in the centre of the X.

6. Push the pin into a pencil rubber.

7. Hold the pencil up and count the turns in one minute.

The faster the cups turn, the windier it is!

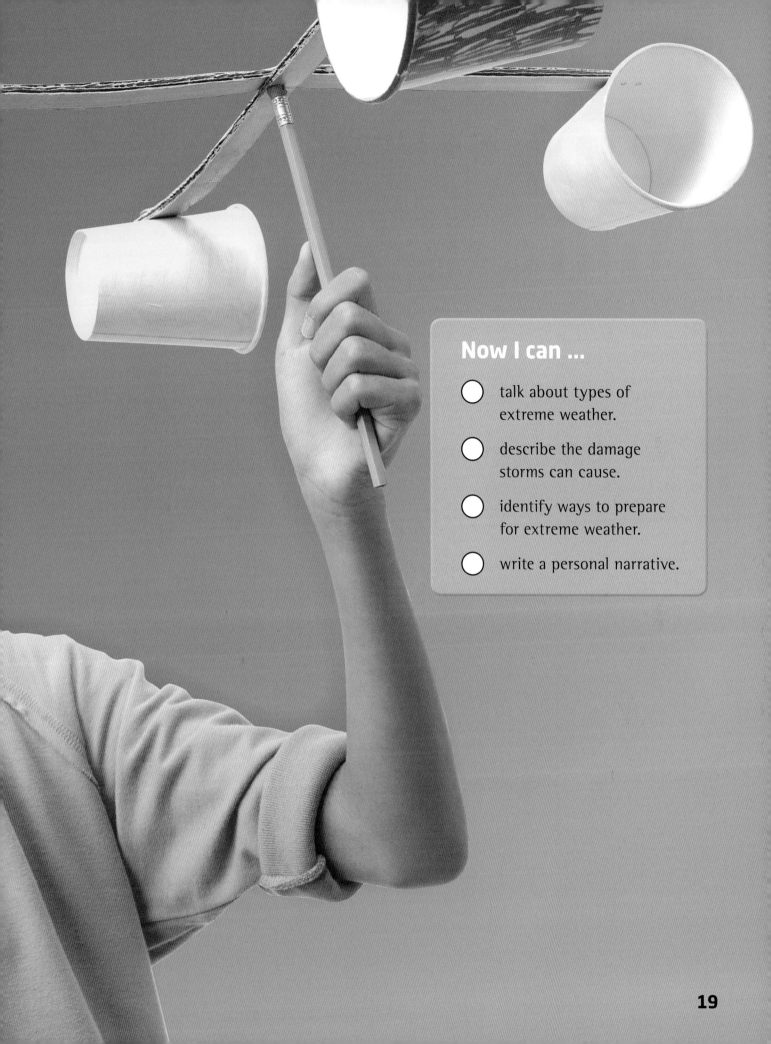

Now I can ...

- ○ talk about types of extreme weather.
- ○ describe the damage storms can cause.
- ○ identify ways to prepare for extreme weather.
- ○ write a personal narrative.

Unit 2

Copycat Animals

In this unit, I will ...
- describe animal features.
- describe how animals protect themselves.
- talk about ways animals imitate others.
- write a paragraph of classification.

Tick T for *True* or F for *False*.

1. This is a plant.   (T) (F)

2. It's very soft.   (T) (F)

3. It's very small.   (T) (F)

4. It's got sharp teeth.   (T) (F)

Allied cowrie,
Papua New Guinea

Some animals can look like other animals or even like a plant! These copycats are trying to hide from, or trick, a hungry **predator**. They can look like another more dangerous animal or like another animal the predator does not like eating.

spots

a predator

This cheetah's black **spots** act as **camouflage**. This way, the cheetah does not **frighten** its **prey** when it is time to **hunt**.

a stripe

This colourful frog has **stripes** on its skin. The bright colours tell hungry predators that the frog is **poisonous**.

prey

These butterflies are not the same **species**, but they **resemble** each other. The top one tastes horrible. The other one **copies** its shape and colours and tastes horrible, too.

This **insect** is as green as a leaf. It **imitates** the **characteristics** of colour and shape of leaves to help it **hide** from predators.

3 **Work with a friend.** What did you learn? Ask and answer.

How do you know which frogs are poisonous?

They've got stripes and bright colours.

23

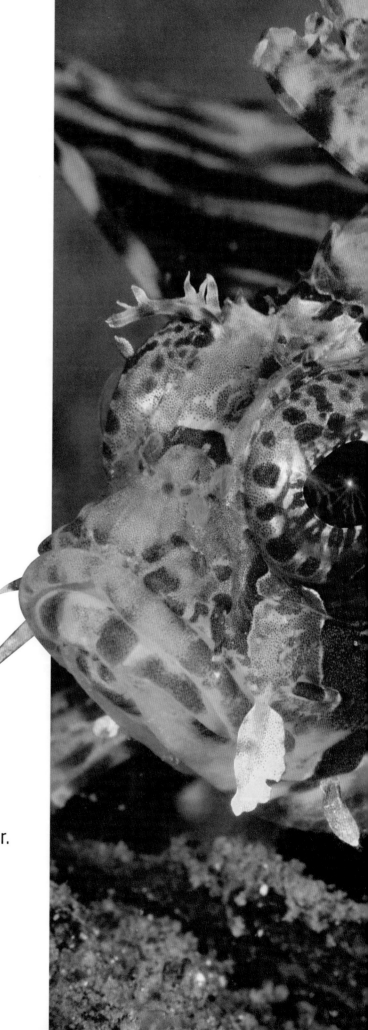

It's a Wild World

It's a wild world!
It's hard work staying alive.
Animals do amazing things
in order to survive.

An insect that looks like a leaf
copies plants to be free.
Predators are everywhere,
and looking for a feast!

CHORUS

Camouflage and imitate.
Resemble and escape.
Animals hide in front of our eyes, every day.

The hunter and the hunted,
predator and prey,
must hunt or hide to stay alive,
each and every day.

A pretty frog can be
as deadly as a poisonous snake.
It's got stripes to tell
its enemies to stay away!

CHORUS

It's a wild world!

5 **Work with a friend.** Ask and answer.

1. What predators have you seen?
2. What is their prey?
3. How does the prey avoid the predators?

Lionfish, Indonesia

That katydid is **as green as** the leaf it sits on.
That butterfly is not **as pretty as** the blue one.
Poison dart frogs are **as dangerous as** some snakes.

6 **Read and write.** Work with a friend. Take turns. Compare.

1. some insects / thin / sticks

Some insects are as thin as sticks. _____

2. a polar bear / white / snow

_____

3. king snakes / not dangerous / coral snakes

_____

4. a bee sting / bad / a wasp sting

_____

5. a lion / not loud / a howler monkey

_____

a bee

a wasp

7 **Compare the animals.** Choose one word from each group. Make sentences.

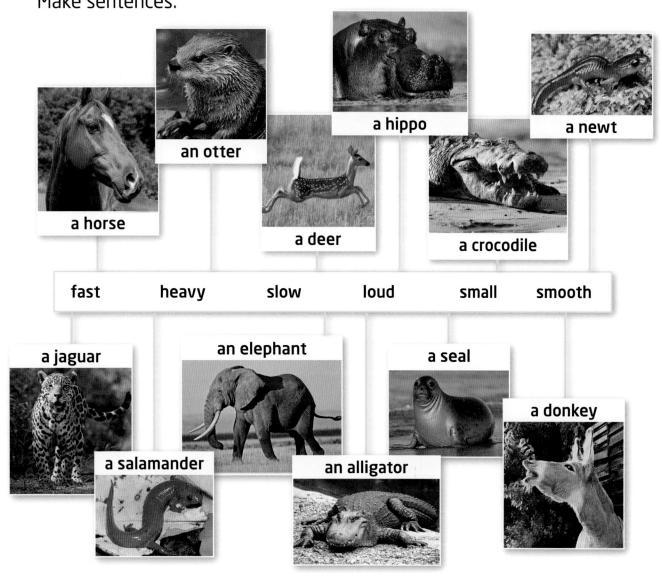

a hippo

a newt

an otter

a horse

a deer

a crocodile

fast   heavy   slow   loud   small   smooth

a jaguar

an elephant

a seal

a donkey

a salamander

an alligator

8 **Work in a group.** Take turns. Make sentences. Use the last word in each sentence to start the next sentence.

The hippo is as big as the car.

The car is as green as the frog.

The frog is as funny as you. Ha ha!

9 **Listen and repeat.** Then, read and write. TR: A14

The butterfly fish **confuses** its predators with a spot like an eye.

The jaguar **attacks**.

The cobra **defends** itself. The mongoose **avoids** its bite.

The deer **escapes** by running away.

1. All predators _____ *attack* _____ prey.

2. Bluebirds _____ their eggs from predators.

3. The tails of Calabar Pythons look like heads. This _____ predators so that they will not know where to strike!

4. Some animals use camouflage to _____ predators.

5. A rabbit that runs fast can _____ the coyote that chases it.

10 **Listen.** Stick *True* or *False*. Work with a friend. Compare your answers. TR: A15

> The spot on the tail looks like an eye. The sentence is true.

> You're right! My turn.

The jaguar **is** dangerous, **isn't it**?
Those snakes **are** scary, **aren't they**?
This insect **looks** like a stick, **doesn't it**?
Giraffes **don't** eat meat, **do they**?
It**'s got** a big nose, **hasn't it**?

That frog **wasn't** poisonous, **was it**?
The cat **escaped** from the dog, **didn't it**?
The dogs **were** loud, **weren't they**?
The cats **weren't** friendly, **were they**?
They**'ve got** long ears, **haven't they**?

11 **Read.** Complete the sentences.

1. The katydid is pretending it's a leaf, _____ isn't it? _____?

2. The donkey doesn't look thirsty, _____?

3. That python really confused its predator, _____?

4. Cats like sleeping in the sun, _____?

5. Baby penguins are so lovely, _____?

6. Those weren't copycat animals, _____?

7. This lion's got big teeth, _____?

12 **Play a game.** Cut out the question tags on page 163.
Listen. Which tag completes the sentence? Glue nine to complete
your game. TR: A17

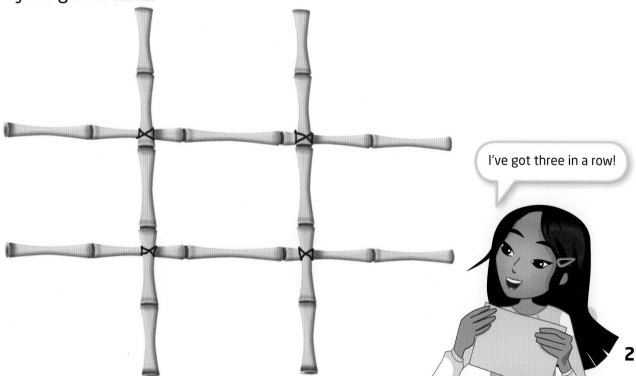

I've got three in a row!

Copycat Animals

The leafy sea dragon is a weird but beautiful copycat. From its name you would think it imitates a dragon, wouldn't you? But it only gets that name from its funny shape. The leafy sea dragon imitates what is around it. It lives in seaweed, and so its body looks like a piece of seaweed. The sea dragon imitates the shape and colour of seaweed, and it even looks like floating seaweed when it moves. It doesn't use the parts of its body that look like seaweed to swim. It uses fins that are transparent, so it's hard to see them move.

The leafy sea dragon not only looks like a copycat, it also dances like a copycat. A male and female sea dragon will copy each other's movements for hours!

The mimic octopus is the only sea creature that can imitate many different species. It not only changes its colour, it also changes its shape. It has arms as thick as pencils. When it spreads them wide, they look like the spines of a lionfish. It can hide some of its arms in the sand, and leave two arms out. Then, with its white and brown stripes and the two arms, it looks like a sea snake! It can also pull its arms together and swim on the sea floor so, to a predator, it looks like a poisonous flatfish!

Like other octopuses, the mimic octopus has eight arms and three hearts. It swims by shooting out jets of water through a siphon. It also has a large brain for its size. What a clever octopus!

One kind of spider tricks predators by imitating an ant. It holds two legs up to look more like an ant when it walks.

A mimic octopus imitating a poisonous flatfish.

leafy sea dragon

14 **Read and write.** Work with a friend. Compare your answers.

1. What does the leafy sea dragon imitate? _____

2. What does the leafy sea dragon use to swim? _____

3. What does the mimic octopus look like? _____

4. What does the mimic octopus do with its arms? _____

15 **Work with a friend.** Choose the leafy sea dragon or the mimic octopus to talk about. Your friend will listen and complete the first row. Then listen to your friend and complete the second row.

Habitat	Shape	Colour	Movement

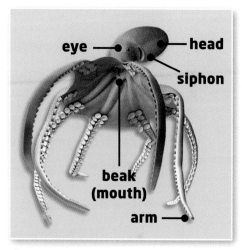

An octopus

16 **Work in groups of three.** Take turns. Summarise the reading.

Paragraphs of Classification

A paragraph of classification describes characteristics that members of a group share. You can define, compare and contrast details to show how things belong to a group or class. You can use words such as *both*, *each of*, *like*, *but* and *unlike*.

17 **Read.** Read about two types of copycat animals. How does the writer classify them? What words does the writer use to show their characteristics? Underline the words and expressions.

One or two ways to imitate

Some animals copy other animals to avoid attack. They copy the things that predators avoid, such as a bad taste or a dangerous weapon. Some species copy the appearance of another animal, but not its other characteristics. For example, the viceroy and the soldier butterfly resemble each other. They also both taste horrible to predators. These types of animals imitate in two ways. The ash borer moth looks like a wasp, but it does not have a sting. Predators avoid it, but it can't sting them. The ash borer moth belongs to the class of animals that only copies appearance.

viceroy butterfly

ash borer moth

18 **Write.** Write about animals that belong to a certain group or class. Describe the characteristics that they share.

19 **Work in a small group.** Share your writing.

32

NATIONAL GEOGRAPHIC
Mission

Protect biodiversity.

- Why is it important to protect diverse species of animals?

- How does biodiversity affect your community?

- Work in a small group. Discuss a local species of animal. Think of ways to protect it. Discuss and write the best ideas in the box.

'*We need to increase people's interest and awareness about wildlife and conservation issues, and reduce the general disconnection from nature.*'

Krithi Karanth
Conservation Biologist
Emerging Explorer

We can tell people about the animal.

_____

_____

_____

_____

- Work with another group. Share your ideas. Are they the same or different? Which ideas does everyone like best?

A tarsier

20 **Make a classroom collage.**

1. Work in small groups. Choose a habitat such as a sea, a forest or a desert.

2. Discuss how animals protect themselves in that place.

3. In your part of the collage, show some animals that use camouflage and some that survive in other ways.

There is a leaf-tailed gecko on a tree trunk in the rainforest. It uses camouflage to survive. Can you see it?

AGE IN THE RAINFOREST

Now I can ...

- ⬤ describe animal features.

- ⬤ describe how animals protect themselves.

- ⬤ talk about ways animals imitate other animals.

- ⬤ write a paragraph of classification.

Unit 3
Music in Our World

In this unit, I will ...
- identify musical instruments.
- talk about musical styles.
- express preferences.
- write a paragraph of contrast.

Circle the correct answer.

1. The man is holding

   a. a hunting tool.

   b. a musical instrument.

2. He is playing

   a. traditional music.

   b. classical music.

Makena Beach, Maui

1 **Listen and read.** TR: A19

2 **Listen and repeat.** TR: A20

There are three main types of musical instruments. Stringed instruments make music when you pluck the strings. Wind instruments make sounds when you blow air into them. Percussion instruments make different sounds when you hit them or shake them.

Music has its own language. Each single sound is a **note**. Play two notes or more at one time to make a **chord**. A string of notes and chords played one after the other makes a **melody**. The thump, thump, thump that makes you want to dance is the **beat**. Combine them all, slow and fast over time, and you have **rhythm**.

a violin

a saxophone

a piano

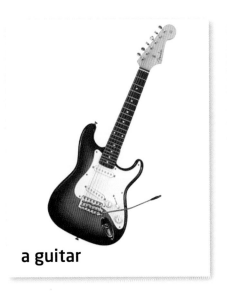
a guitar

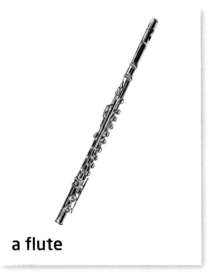
a flute

a drum

Do you want your **band** to play better? You have to **practise**! Play songs again and again until they sound really good. When your band sounds good, you can **perform** for an audience. Invite your friends to the **concert**! If you don't play an instrument but you have a good voice, you could be the **lead singer**!

3 **Work with a friend.** What did you learn? Ask and answer.

How many types of instruments are there?

There are three main types.

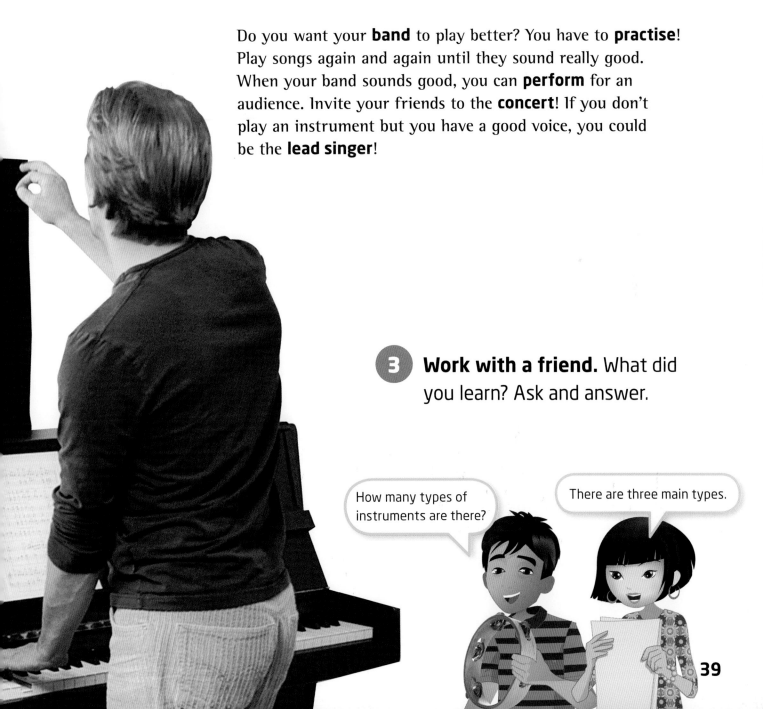

4 Listen, read and sing. TR: A21

Music Is Fun

Have you ever listened to hip-hop?
Have you ever listened to drums?
I listen to all kinds of music.
It's amazing fun.

Listen to the saxophone.
Listen to the beat.
Listen to the melody.
Feel it in your feet!

The flute is playing.
The piano is, too.
I can hear the guitar.
Can you?

CHORUS

Listen to the rhythm.
Listen to that band!
Sing the notes (la, la, la)
and clap your hands.

Have you ever played a note?
Have you ever played a chord?
Have you ever played a rhythm:
1, 2, 3, 4?

CHORUS

5 Work with a friend. Ask and answer.

1. Who are your favourite musicians?

2. What instruments do they play?

3. Why do you like their music?

4. Do you play a musical instrument?

Drummers, Ninga, Burundi

Have you ever **listened** to hip-hop?   Yes, I **have**.

Have you ever **danced** to hip-hop?   No, I **haven't**.

Have you ever **been** to a concert?   No, I **never have**.

Has Lisa **ever heard** an orchestra perform?   No, she **has never heard** an orchestra perform.

6 **Read.** Complete the sentences.

1. This song is new. I _____have never heard_____ (hear) it before.

2. I _____ (go) to see an opera. I don't think I'd like it.

3. _____ (listen to) jazz? Yes, I like it!

4. If you _____ (hear) her sing, then you know she sings well.

5. This is his first time. He _____ (perform) in public.

6. _____ you _____ (dance) to a slow song?

Chinese opera

42

7 **What about you?** Write questions. Work with a friend. Answer each other's questions.

1. go / rock concert _____ *Have you ever been to a rock concert?* _____

2. play / a musical instrument _____

3. have / music lessons _____

4. see / a band _____

5. listen to / classical music _____

6. sing / in public _____

7. hear / your brother sing _____

8. perform / in public _____

8 **Work in groups of three.** Use words from the list to ask and answer. Take turns.

band	guitar	dance	play
concert	piano	have jazz lessons	sing
drums	saxophone	listen to	see
famous	singer	meet	

Have you ever heard your sister sing?

Of course I've heard her sing! She's good.

9 **Listen and repeat.** Then read and write. TR: A23

hip-hop

classical

pop

jazz

rock

1. A large orchestra that includes cellos, violins, a piano, double bass and trumpets

   often plays _____ classical _____ music.

2. Some music uses spoken words instead of singing.

   It's called _____.

3. A type of music with swing and rhythm that began 100 years ago and had

   links to the music of West Africa is _____.

4. This music is made for lots of people to enjoy. It's easy to listen to.

   It's _____ music.

5. We call this music with a strong beat and fast rhythm _____.

10 **Work with a friend.** Talk and stick. Put the types of music in order
(1 = most favourite). Discuss your favourite music and give examples
of songs and performers.

1 2 3 4 5

He sings **more loudly than** me.   She plays the violin **better than** he does.
I play the guitar **as well as** my brother.   He practises the piano **less often than** me.

11 **Read and write.** Make comparisons. Use five words from the list.

> beautifully   fast   hard   often   slow   well   worse

1. He's good. He plays the guitar _____more often than_____ he plays the drums.

2. That's not good. The orchestra sounds _____ the band.

3. She practises _____ than he does. She plays at least

   twice a day.

4. I dance to hip-hop _____ I dance to rock.

5. I play the piano _____ my older sister.

12 **Play a game.** Play with a friend.
Take turns. Spin and make
sentences with a comparison.

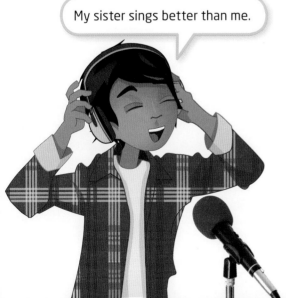

My sister sings better than me.

45

It's All Music

People made music before they could write about it. The oldest instrument ever found is more than 35,000 years old. It's a flute. Instruments of this type are called wind instruments. Like the sound of the wind, the music comes from moving air. Some wind instruments have a special piece for your mouth. The piece also helps to make the sound. Each instrument has a shape that makes its sound different. Some wind instruments have holes for fingers. Others have buttons to press. Holes and buttons let you change the way the air travels to change the melody.

Another way to make music is with strings. When you slide a finger over a string, or pluck it, it makes music. Most stringed instruments have thick or thin strings, and long or short strings, to make different notes.

The shape of the body of a stringed instrument also helps to make the sound. Musicians use a bow to play some stringed instruments. The bow is a piece of wood with hairs or a string stretched between its ends.

You can also make music by hitting or shaking something that makes a sound. Percussion instruments can be made from many things. That's because most things make a sound when you hit them. An empty space inside the instrument makes the sound louder. Percussion instruments with strings make music when the strings are hit. A drum is a percussion instrument. A piano is a percussion instrument, too. When piano keys are pressed, hammers inside the piano hit the strings to make music.

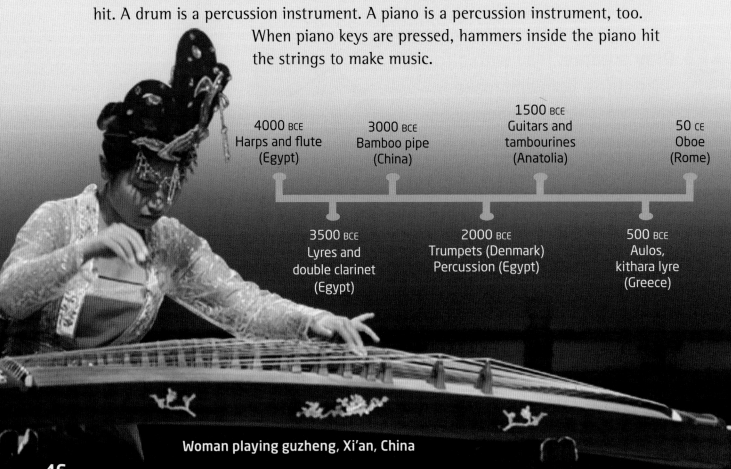

4000 BCE
Harps and flute
(Egypt)

3000 BCE
Bamboo pipe
(China)

1500 BCE
Guitars and
tambourines
(Anatolia)

50 CE
Oboe
(Rome)

3500 BCE
Lyres and
double clarinet
(Egypt)

2000 BCE
Trumpets (Denmark)
Percussion (Egypt)

500 BCE
Aulos,
kithara lyre
(Greece)

Woman playing guzheng, Xi'an, China

14 Choose the best answer.

1. A drum is a _____.

   a. stringed instrument   b. percussion instrument   c. wind instrument

2. If you press a key on a wind instrument, the sound changes because _____.

   a. your finger is heavy

   b. it holds the instrument tightly

   c. the path for the air changes

3. An empty space inside percussion instruments makes the sound _____.

   a. softer   b. faster   c. louder

4. Some stringed instruments are played with a _____.

   a. bow   b. hammer   c. key

15 Match the instruments and their types. Work with a friend.
Tick the correct column.

	Wind	Stringed	Percussion
Drums			
Flute			
Guitar			
Piano			
Saxophone			
Violin			

Mozart composed his first song when he was four years old.

16 Work in groups of three. Invent a unique band that mixes different musical instruments. What six instruments would you choose?

Paragraphs of Contrast

Paragraphs of contrast show the differences between things. You can use facts and descriptive details to contrast different characteristics. You can also use words like *but*, *although*, *unlike*, *while*, *instead* and *in contrast* to show things are not the same.

17 **Read.** Read the paragraphs about two ways to compose music. How does the writer show they are different? Underline the words used.

Composing, then and now

In the past, composers traditionally created their music with paper and pen. But now, technology – such as computers and phone apps – is changing how music is made. Although some composers still write by hand, more and more are using these new tools. Before, a composer would write notes on lined measures of music. In contrast, apps let the composer hum a melody and then the apps write the musical notes!

Many people think that composing music was more difficult in the past. When composers wanted to make changes as they wrote, they had to stop and rub out the notes. It was a slow, messy process. Some new apps, unlike old rubbers, make making corrections easy. These apps can show music as a moving stream of colour. To make changes, the composer can pull and twist the music with his or her fingers on the screen. While traditional composers are busy cleaning ink from their fingers, modern composers can write more songs instead!

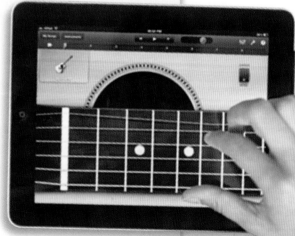

18 **Write.** Write about two styles of music or two musical instruments. How are they different? Use words and expressions that show contrast.

19 **Work in a small group.** Share your writing.

Mission

Change through music.

- Work with a friend. How does music change how you think and feel? How can music make the world a better place?

- Choose a song that changed how you think. Write some words from the song in the box.

'Music can change the world. It can inspire people to care, to do something positive, to make a difference.'

Jack Johnson
National Geographic Arts Ambassador
for the Environment

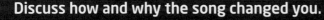

Music can make people feel happy.

- Discuss how and why the song changed you.

20 Make an instrument.

1. Work in small groups and research home-made musical instruments.

2. Collect recycling and make a musical instrument.

3. Join other groups with instruments and practise together.

4. Have a concert!

We made percussion and wind instruments. They sound great!

Now I can ...

○ identify musical instruments.

○ talk about musical styles.

○ express preferences.

○ write a paragraph of contrast.

1 **Carla is doing a survey about music.** What are her questions? What do Laura and Andrew answer? Complete the table. TR: A26

Questions	Laura	Andrew
1.	hip-hop	
2.		
3.		He likes singing. He sang in public once.
4.	none	

2 **Do a survey.** Ask two other students the same questions. Make notes.

3 **Work in groups of three.** One of you is going on holiday to a place with extreme weather. How are you going to prepare? Take turns to ask questions and give advice.

hurricane
sandstorm
flood
hailstorm
heatwave
ever
blizzard
never
tornado
plan
tropical storm

I'm going to Antarctica! That's amazing, isn't it? Have you ever been there?

I'm going to take very warm gloves!

No, I've never been there. What are you going to pack?

If you go to Antarctica, you need more than warm gloves!

4 **Match the copycat animal.** Find the photo that matches the text.

gecko mantid tawny frogmouth

1. This animal's skin is as rough as a tree. And it is brown like a tree, too! That helps it hide from predators.

2. This animal has feathers as brown as the colour of wood. If it hears you, it does not move. It makes its body stiff. It looks just like a branch!

3. This animal imitates the colour of a dead leaf. It uses the leaf as camouflage. Even if you look for it, you will never see it!

5 **Continue the story.** Work in groups of four. Choose a story. Read it aloud. Then, add your own sentence to the story. Take turns. Then share your story with another group.

1

It is raining hard. Paolo runs under a tree. Maria is standing there, too. They can hear thunder. Then, there is a flash of lightning! Maria says ...

2

A few friends met to play music. Paolo is good at playing the guitar. Maria has a beautiful voice. Alba has a drum. They talk about what music to play.

_____

_____

_____

_____

Let's Talk

It's my turn.

I will ...
• take turns.
• give commands.
• talk about who won a game.

1 **Listen and read.** TR: A27

Marco: **Whose turn is it?**
Amy: It's my turn.
Marco: Well, **hurry up!**

Amy: **Yes, I won!**
Marco: Now **we're tied.**
Amy: **No!** What do you mean?
Marco: Well, I won last time!

Whose turn is it? It's my turn. It's his/her turn.	Hurry up! Come on!	Yes, I won! We're tied. Sorry, you lost!	No! That's not true. That's not possible.

2 **Work with a friend.** Use the table. Take turns to talk about playing a game.

Who's going to make notes?

3 **Listen and read.** TR: A28

Sonia: So, I'll be the reporter. **Who's going to** make notes?

Olga: **I'll do that.**

Sonia: Thanks. **Can you** watch the time, Hans?

Hans: OK. Er, **what page are we on**?

Olga: **We're on page** 25. We're sharing ideas about music.

Hans: Thanks, Olga.

Who's going to _____? Can you _____?	**I'll do that.** I'll (watch the time). I'll be _____. I can _____.	**What page are we on?** Which page is it?	**We're on page** _____.
		How long have we got?	We've got _____.
		What are we doing?	We're _____.

4 **Listen to two discussions.** Circle what the students are doing. TR: A29

1. They are a. doing a role play.   b. doing a crossword.   c. making a poster.

2. They are a. doing a role play.   b. doing a crossword.   c. making a poster.

5 **Work in groups of three.** Prepare and practise discussions. Choose one task. Discuss how you are going to do it.

1. Make a musical instrument from recycled objects.

2. Make a collage about copycat animals.

3. Make a poster about the weather.

Unit 4

Life Out There

In this unit, I will ...
- discuss life in space.
- discuss space exploration.
- express my opinion.
- write a persuasive paragraph.

Circle the correct letter.

1. What are they looking at?

   a. the clouds   b. the stars

2. What time of day is it?

   a. late   b. the middle
      afternoon   of the night

3. Why are they wearing coats?

   a. They are   b. It is cold.
      on the moon.

The Milky Way

Earth is a **planet** that moves around the Sun. Other planets also **orbit** the Sun. The Sun and planets make up our **solar system**. The Sun is a star like the stars that you see in the sky at night. Some stars have solar systems with planets, too. There may be another planet out there that has an **atmosphere** with oxygen to breathe.

A star and the planets that orbit around it make up a solar system. Stars and solar systems make up a **galaxy**. Our galaxy is called the Milky Way. It has about a 100 billion stars. Outside our galaxy, there are more galaxies! There are more galaxies in the **universe** than there are stars in a galaxy. How many? We don't know! There are too many, and lots are too far away to see.

an orbit

a planet

A **comet** is a cloud of rock, ice and gas that orbits the Sun. Many earth years pass during its **journey** around the Sun. Scientists keep **data** on comets to know when they will appear.

space

a comet

a galaxy

Think of the many galaxies in the universe. Think of the many stars in each galaxy. Think of the many planets that orbit the stars. Do you think that **extraterrestrials** may live on one of the planets? Many people **debate** this question.

3 **Work with a friend.** What did you learn? Discuss.

I don't think there's life on other planets.

Well, I think it's possible.

4 **Listen, read and sing.** TR: A32

Deep in Outer Space

*Let's all go on a journey
through the atmosphere.
Beyond our solar system,
far away from here.*

*We might find a new planet.
We might find a new place.
We might find things we've never seen,
deep in outer space.*

**Deep in outer space,
who knows what we might find?
Deep in outer space,
deep in outer space.**

*Somewhere in the universe,
we might find a moon
where flowers grow.
You never know,
but I wish we'd get there soon!*

CHORUS

*But right here on planet Earth
life is all around.
Our world is full of colour,
texture, light and sound.*

*We can go on a journey
right outside our door,
and see the wonders of life on Earth
and so much more.*

CHORUS

Deep in outer space.

5 **Work with a friend.** Talk about life
in outer space. Take turns.

- moon
- planet
- solar system
- universe

60

Rosette Nebula

If a planet has an atmosphere, it **may** have life.	Do you think astronauts **might** go to the moon again?
There **might** be life on other planets.	Yes, but it **may** be very simple life.

6 **Read.** Tick the true sentences.

1. Some stars may have planets like Earth.   ✓

2. We may find extraterrestrials on a distant planet.   ☐

3. A meteor might hit Earth.   ☐

4. The Milky Way might be a galaxy.   ☐

5. Earth may have an atmosphere.   ☐

6. You may become an astronaut.   ☐

7 **Complete the sentences.**

are	is	live
may be	may discover	may live

1. There _____ _may be_ _____ oxygen on planets in other galaxies.

2. There _____ no oxygen on the Moon.

3. Extraterrestrials _____ on other planets.

4. Astronauts _____ in the space station for some time.

5. There _____ other solar systems in the universe.

6. One day, scientists _____ life on other planets.

62

8 **What do you think?** Write sentences.

1. extraterrestrial / green skin Extraterrestrials might not have green skin like they
do in films.

2. comet / lifetime _____

_____

3. universe / galaxies _____

_____

4. comet / our planet _____

_____

5. find / life _____

_____

9 **Work in groups of three.** Take turns. Make a sentence about life in the universe. Your friends will add more information.

There may be another planet with an atmosphere like Earth's.

The planet might be too hot or too cold for life.

If the planet has water, it may have plants.

10 **Listen and repeat.** Then read and write. TR: A34

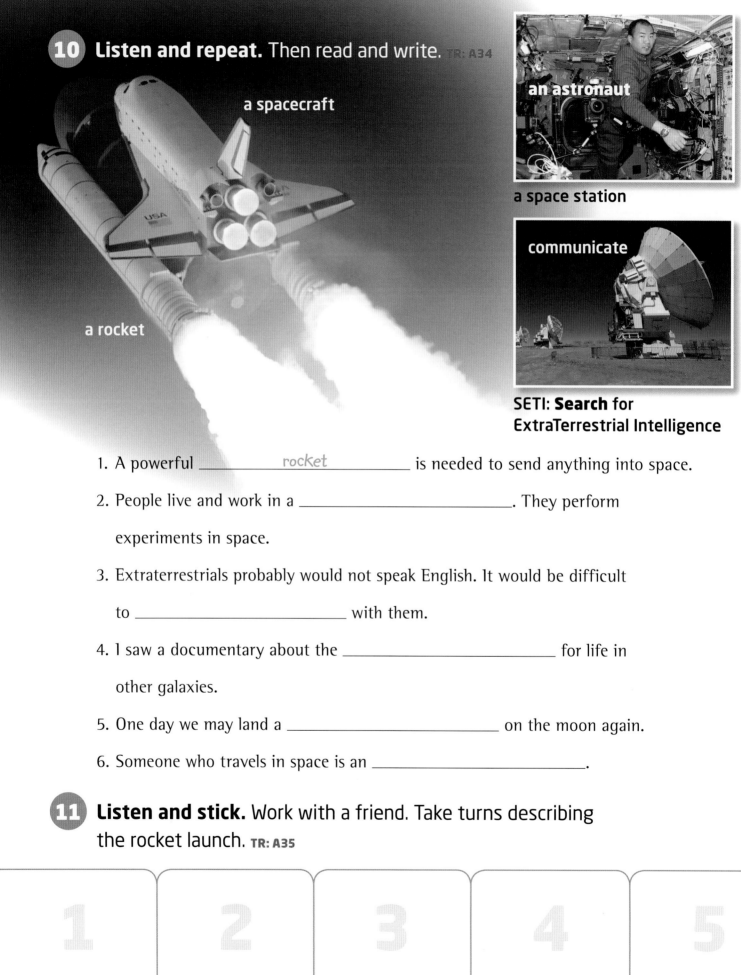

a spacecraft

an astronaut

a space station

communicate

a rocket

SETI: **Search** for **ExtraTerrestrial Intelligence**

1. A powerful _____ rocket _____ is needed to send anything into space.

2. People live and work in a _____. They perform

   experiments in space.

3. Extraterrestrials probably would not speak English. It would be difficult

   to _____ with them.

4. I saw a documentary about the _____ for life in

   other galaxies.

5. One day we may land a _____ on the moon again.

6. Someone who travels in space is an _____.

11 **Listen and stick.** Work with a friend. Take turns describing
the rocket launch. TR: A35

1   2   3   4   5

Did **everyone** see that comet?
Someone will go to Mars one day.

Does **anyone** want to be an astronaut?
No one can see all the stars in the universe.

12 **Read and write.** Complete the paragraph.

anyone   everyone   no one   someone

_____Everyone_____ likes to debate about life on other planets.

_____ knows for sure if there is life out there, or not. If

_____ tells you that they know, that person really doesn't know!

Are you _____ who likes to debate? I will debate about life in

space with _____ who wants to. _____ knows the

answer, but _____ has an opinion!

13 **Work with a friend.** What about you?

1. Does anyone in your family think there is life on other planets?
2. Name one thing everyone in your family does believe.
3. Name one thing no one in your family believes.
4. Name a funny habit someone in your family has.

14 **Play a game.** Cut out the cards on page 165. Make sentences.
Take turns.

Everyone here is a good student.

Someone in this class is wearing an orange T-shirt.

Has anyone got an umbrella?

Listening for Life

If extraterrestrials live on other planets, we can't see them. Planets in other solar systems are very far away. We can't see the planets, even with our biggest telescopes. But what if the extraterrestrials want to communicate with us? What if they are sending us messages? This signal would travel through space. After many years, it might reach our solar system. The signal would be very weak. It would be hidden in the noise from other places in space. We would need special tools to hear it.

Scientists at SETI have made a tool for listening. It uses 42 satellite dishes that are joined together. Scientists plan to have 350 dishes one day. They point all the dishes at the same place in the sky. Then they search for any data they can hear. The dishes can hear very weak signals. For example, they could hear a mobile phone on a planet in our solar system. (That's if anyone had a mobile phone on Jupiter!) The dishes pick up noise from radios on Earth, too. Scientists must be careful to avoid this noise.

We have not heard from an extraterrestrial yet. But is it possible that they are listening to us? If they are, most could not have heard us yet. We have used radios for fewer than 100 years. That isn't much time for the big distances in the universe. In that time, our signal could only reach a small number of stars Extraterrestrials from nearby solar systems would not hear us for thousands of years.

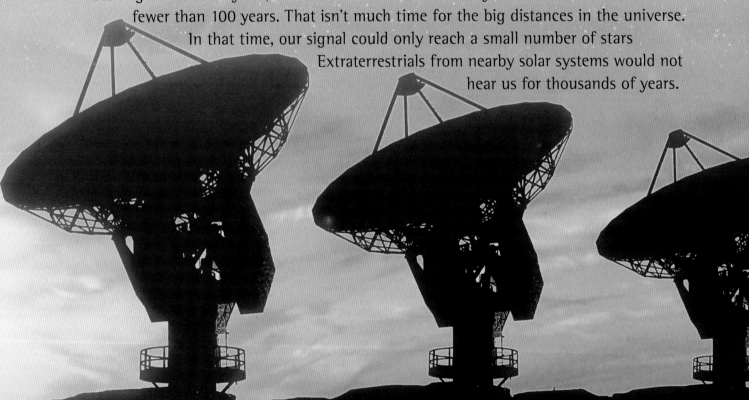

Length of Time Needed for Radio Waves to Reach Earth

4.3 light years	431 light years	27,000 light years
Earth Nearest star, Alpha Centauri	North Pole star, Polaris	The centre of the Milky Way

16 **Tick T for *True* or F for *False*.**

1. Extraterrestrials have listened to our radio waves for over 100 years. (T) (F)

2. SETI dishes listen for life by listening for radio signals. (T) (F)

3. Scientists point the SETI dishes in lots of directions. (T) (F)

4. Radio waves from Earth are a problem for SETI scientists. (T) (F)

17 **Should we search for life?** Write why and why not.

I think it's a good idea to search for life because ...	I think it's a bad idea to search for life because ...

18 **Work with a friend.** Look at the table and discuss. Support your opinion.

The first astronauts were fruit flies. They were launched on 20th February 1947.

I think it's a good thing to search for life because we can learn lots of things from extraterrestrials.

But how would we communicate with them?

2,480,000 light years

13,100,000,000 light years

The nearest galaxy, Andromeda

As far as we can see in the universe

67

Paragraphs of Persuasion

In persuasive paragraphs, you write to convince the reader of your opinion. To persuade the reader, you use facts to support your opinion. Write strong sentences that show you believe in what you are saying. Introduce your facts with expressions such as *research shows*, *according to* and *the facts show that*.

19 **Read.** How is the writer persuasive? Underline the words.

Forever searching

A long time ago, people thought that the Sun and planets orbited Earth. We like to think that we are at the centre of things! But scientists studied the stars carefully. Their research shows that we are not at the centre. Copernicus was the first to say that Earth orbits the Sun. He was right. And the Sun orbits the centre of the galaxy. The universe has many stars that we can't see. And according to some NASA scientists, somewhere there may be life.

Why do we search? The facts show that we have always been people who search. For example, Zheng was an explorer from China who travelled as far as Arabia and the Horn of Africa in the 1400s. Frederick Cook went to the North Pole in 1908. And Roald Amundsen travelled to the South Pole in 1911. We search on Earth and in space because we like to find answers. And a big question is, are we alone? We will search until we know.

20 **Write.** Do you think we should search for life in space? Take a position. Think about cost, usefulness, urgent problems on Earth and so on. Use facts to persuade.

21 **Work in a small group.** Share your writing.

NATIONAL GEOGRAPHIC
Mission

Be curious.

- Think about things you want to know. How can you find answers?

- Work with a friend. Discuss. Do you search for answers even when it's difficult? How do you feel when you finally find the answer? Write your ideas in the box.

'We finally have the tools and technology to answer this age-old question: Are we alone? Jupiter's moon Europa is a beautiful place to go and explore that question.'

Kevin Hand
Planetary Scientist/Astrobiologist
Emerging Explorer

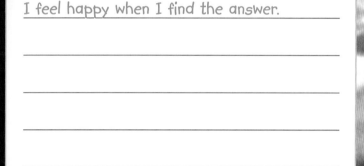

I feel happy when I find the answer.

- Work in a group. Share your ideas. Are they the same or different? Which idea does everyone like best?

Jupiter

Europa

22 **Find information and make a model of a type of place where you think we could find life.**

1. Choose a type of place you think might have life.

2. Find information.

3. Use the information you find and your imagination to recreate the surface of the type of planet or moon you choose. Use cardboard, paper and other materials.

4. Draw different life forms as you imagine them.

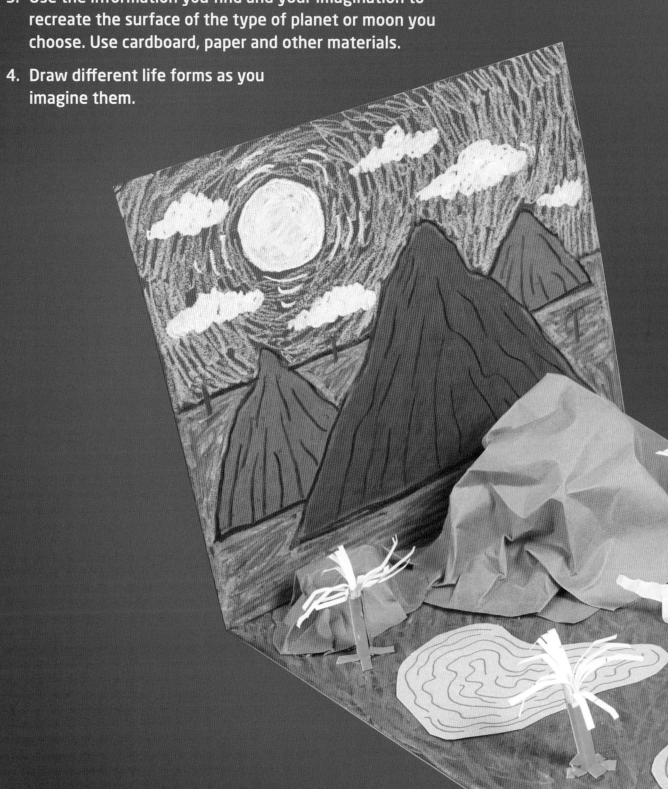

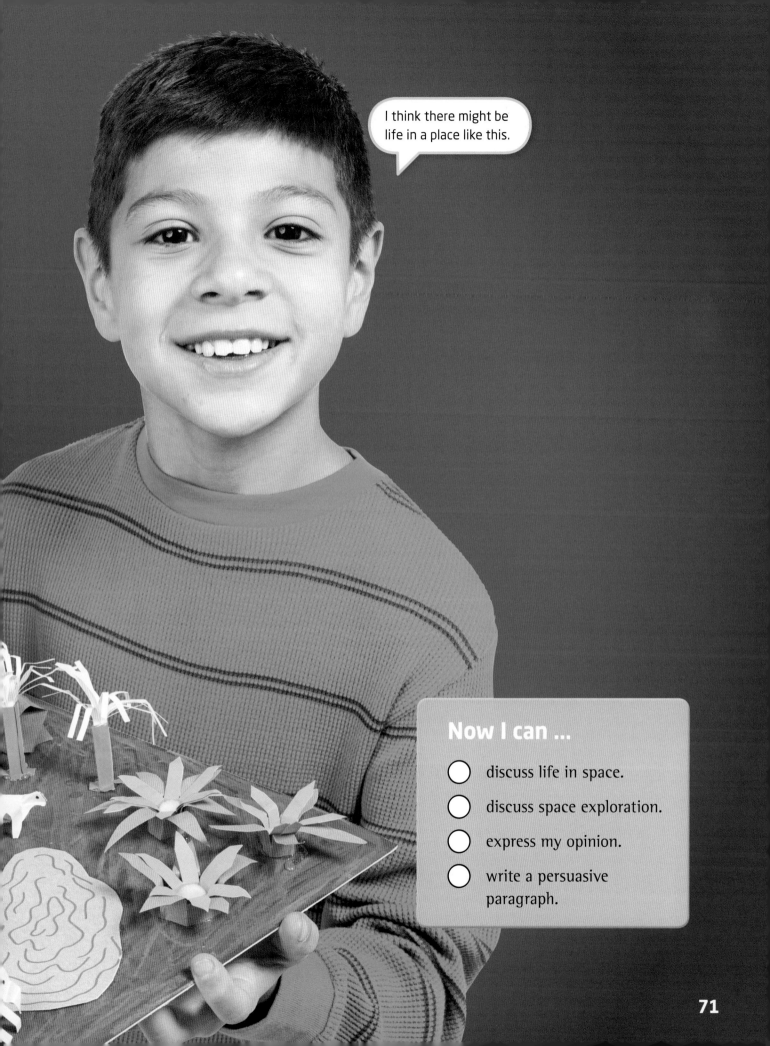

I think there might be life in a place like this.

Now I can ...

- ⚪ discuss life in space.
- ⚪ discuss space exploration.
- ⚪ express my opinion.
- ⚪ write a persuasive paragraph.

Unit 5

Arts Lost and Found

In this unit, I will ...
- talk about why it's good to hold on to traditions.
- explain how the past makes me who I am.
- write a blog.

Look and answer.

1. What is this person wearing?

   a. a hat   b. a mask

2. What is this person doing?

   a. dancing   b. singing

3. Use one word to describe the face.

   _____

Traditional mask dancer, Colombo, Sri Lanka

1 **Listen and read.** TR: A38

2 **Listen and repeat.** TR: A39

Everyone should be **proud** of who they are. What makes you who you are? Part of who you are comes from the past. It comes from the **culture** of your parents, grandparents and people before them. It comes from the **language** you speak, the **art** you see, the stories and music you hear and the **traditions** you **share**.

Dragon boats are a 2,000-year-old Chinese tradition. Racers must co-operate and row together to win. Today, dragon boat racing has become a modern world sport.

Storytelling isn't always done with words. In Laos, dancers tell stories with their hands. The dances are part of their history. This history is **passed down** from one **generation** to the next.

74

The people of Tabasco, Mexico, keep their history alive. This **local** boy has clay on his face. He will do the jaguar dance to bring rain. His people speak an old language that came from the Olmec thousands of years ago.

The people of Ghana **hold on to** their tradition of **weaving** beautiful cloth. **Tourists** come to Ghana to buy cloth. The money that the tourists pay helps the **future** of the **community**.

3 **Work with a friend.** What did you learn? Discuss.

In Laos, they use their hands as part of the dance.

Their hands tell stories.

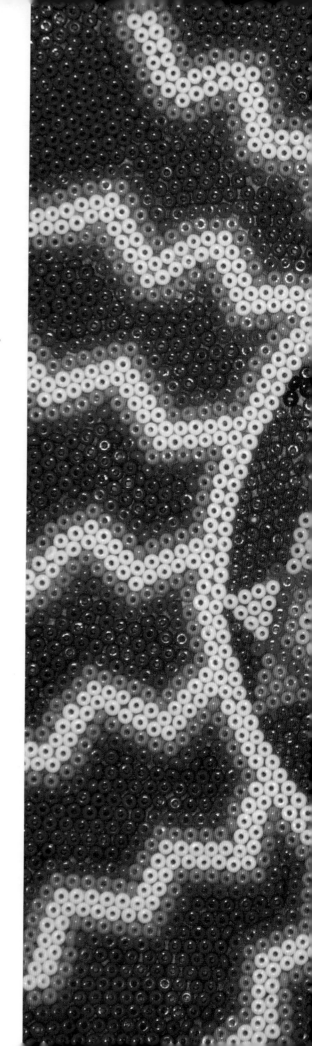

 4 **Listen, read and sing.** TR: A40

Keep Your Culture Strong

Knowing your history is important.
Holding on to your culture is an excellent thing!
Knowing your history is important.
It's up to you to keep your culture strong!

What special art does your culture bring to our world?
What special thing does your family bring to our world?
Weaving? Learn to do it!
Storytelling? Learn to tell it!
What brings your culture pride?

CHORUS

What special art does your culture bring to our world?
What special thing does your family bring to our world?
Embroidery? Learn to sew it!
Sculpture? Learn to sculpt it!
What brings your culture pride?

Your grandparents may seem old to you,
but they know a thing or two!

CHORUS

 **5** **Work with a friend.** Ask and answer.

1. What special art does your culture bring
   to our world?

2. What special thing does your family bring
   to our world?

3. What would you like to learn to do?

76

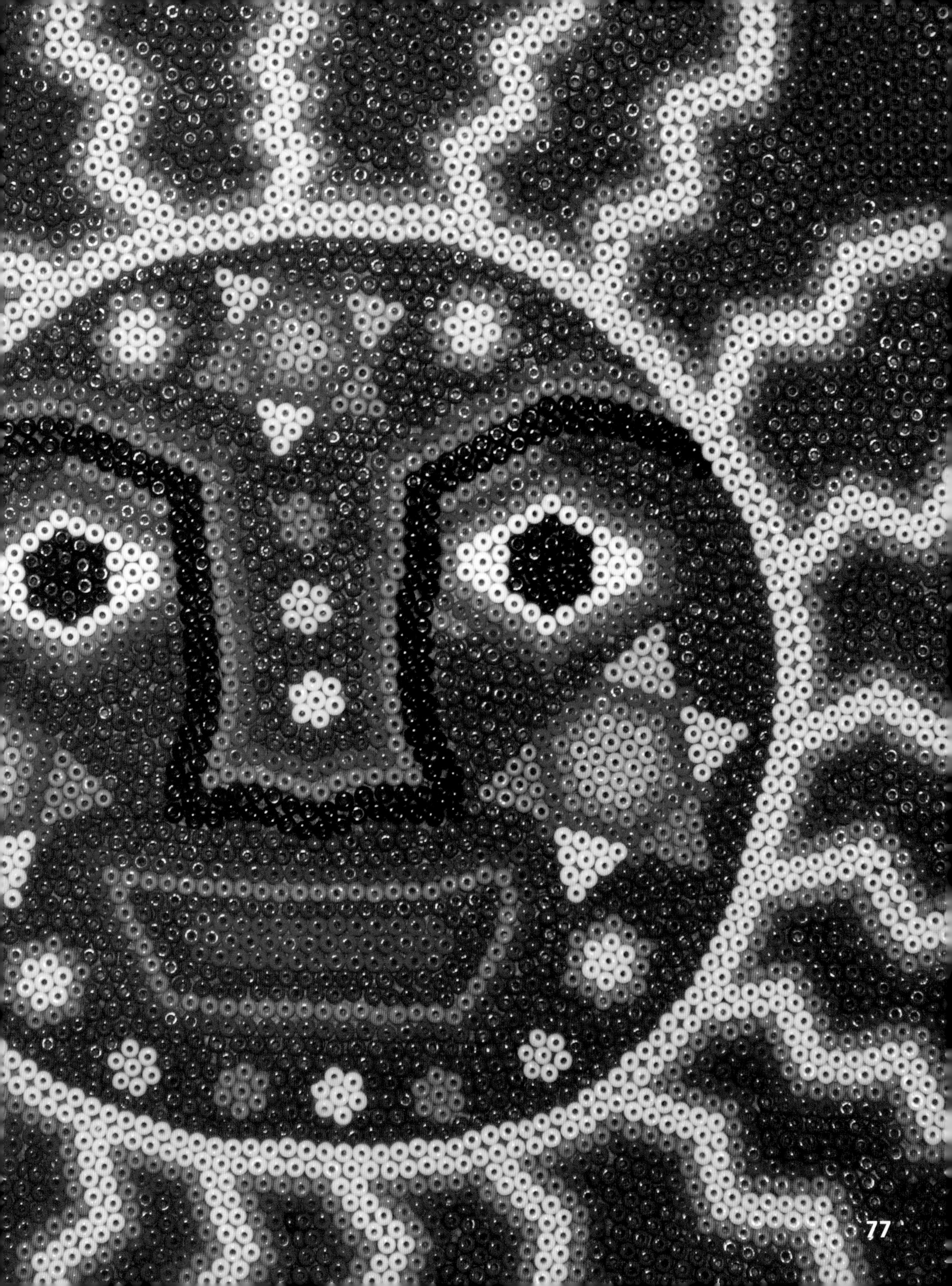

Knowing your history is important.
Holding on to your traditions is a good thing.
Passing down family stories connects generations.
Creating art is a good way to share your culture.

6 **Read.** Complete the sentences. Use the words in the list.

cook   create   paint   row   share   weave

1. _____ Rowing _____ a boat is hard to do without another person.

2. _____ cloth was my grandmother's job.

3. _____ art is exciting!

4. _____ your traditions helps other people

understand you.

5. _____ on wood is fun for people who like colours.

6. _____ traditional recipes is another way to keep

your culture alive.

7 **What about you?** Complete the sentences about you and
your family.

1. Painting _____ is my father's hobby _____.

2. Teaching _____.

3. Cooking _____.

4. Helping _____.

5. Taking photos _____.

6. Reading _____.

8 Complete the conversation.

Mario: Grandpa, did you **listen to music** when you were little?

Grandpa: Yes, I did. ____Listening to music____ was one of my favourite hobbies!

Mario: And did you **go to the cinema**?

Grandpa: Of course! I went every Sunday. _____ was the most important event of the weekend!

Mario: Did you **talk** to your friends **on the phone**?

Grandpa: No, I didn't. _____ was very expensive when I was little!

Mario: And did you **do sport**?

Grandpa: Not really. My parents thought that _____ was a waste of time. They wanted me to study all the time! But I still played football with my friends!

Mario: What about housework? Did you **help around the house**?

Grandpa: Of course! _____ was something everyone had to do!

9 Work in groups of three. Take turns. Express your opinion.

listening to stories	creating art	saving traditions	visiting family
watching dancers	singing traditional songs	looking at old photos	

Looking at my grandfather's old photos is really interesting!

10 Listen and repeat.
Then read and write. TR: A42

handmade

sculpture

embroidery

pottery

jewellery making

1. When a work of art is made by hand, we say it's _____ handmade _____.

2. People use _____ to make their clothes more beautiful and decorative.

3. _____ is made from clay that dries and becomes hard. Sometimes it is heated in an oven.

4. To create a _____, artists can use materials such as wood, stone, metal or ice.

5. _____ is popular. Most children like making bracelets.

11 Look, put in order (1 = most favourite) and stick. Work with a friend. Discuss your preferences.

1 2 3 4 5

My friends are good at **making jewellery**.
I like **eating** traditional foods.
My mother enjoys **embroidering** clothes.
I'm interested in **learning** about new places.

12 **Read and complete the sentences.** Use the words
from the list.

> co-operating   making   passing   sharing   storytelling   travelling

1. Young people today are very interested in _____ sharing _____

   their traditions.

2. I'm very excited about _____ to the country

   of my grandparents.

3. Do you like _____? Storytellers like

   _____ down their traditions.

4. I enjoy _____ traditional jewellery.

5. We can preserve our rich cultural history by _____

   with people from traditional communities.

13 **Play a game.** Cut out the cube on page 167. Work with a friend.
Take turns making sentences.

Playing. I enjoy playing football with my friends.

Brilliant! My turn.

Modern Music with Ancient Roots

Did you know that modern music comes from traditional music? Every generation changes the music from the past. They make it their own. Reggae music began in Jamaica, but it has its roots in African music. Africans came to Jamaica and brought their music. It mixed with music from Europe. Now, reggae has an impact on music all over the world. Dancehall and hip-hop music came from reggae!

Shaabi music is based on Egyptian folk music. It is played with the saxophone and electronic keyboard, which are modern instruments. But it is also played with a kanun, a traditional stringed instrument. The instruments are different, but the musical roots are the same!

Norteño is a modern type of Mexican music with folk-music roots. Old Norteño music was played with an accordion and a Mexican guitar. Then, Norteño bands heard rock music. They added drums, saxophones and electronic keyboards to their bands! Modern Norteño has a stronger beat than the traditional music.

In Japan, many people listen to J-pop music. J-pop is the name for all modern Japanese pop music. It includes many modern music types and instruments like electric guitars and keyboards. In the 1920s, when Japanese pop music began, performers used harmonicas and stringed instruments. The music combined Western jazz and soul with a traditional style of Japanese singing. Today, every J-pop artist or band selects and combines the instruments and music rhythms they like best with their Japanese-language songs.

Mexico - Norteño

Japan - J-pop

Jamaica - Reggae

Egypt - Shaabi

15 Read and write.

1. Where did reggae music begin? _____ Reggae music began in Jamaica.

2. In what country is Norteño performed? _____

3. What kind of music influenced J-pop? _____

4. Which music is based on Egyptian folk music? _____

5. Which music influenced dancehall and hip-hop? _____

16 Compare the music. Work with a friend.

Shaabi

Norteño

electronic Keyboard

J-pop

Mice sing to
each other
at night.

17 Work with a friend. Make new
music. Invent a new musical style.
It can be completely new, or you can
modernise a style you know. What
styles would you mix? What instruments
would you use?

Let's mix tango
and rock!

Yes! We can add drums and an
electric guitar! Any other ideas?

Blog Entries

In a personal blog, you write about your thoughts. You describe what you saw, heard or felt. A blog sounds like an informal conversation. You can ask your readers to post a response to your blog. You can use expressions like *fabulous, brilliant, hated it* and *laugh out loud (lol)*.

18 **Read.** What informal expressions does the writer use in her blog? Underline them.

« » ⊞ 🔊   Cecilia's Blog

The best holiday ever!!!

My family and I went to Machu Picchu in Peru. It was brilliant. First, I went on a long train ride with my family to Aguas Calientes. From there we went on a bus to Machu Picchu. The bus went slowly up the steep mountain. (I'm really glad the bus went slowly!) LOL. From the bus window I saw llamas eating grass.

When we arrived, I was excited. It was fabulous to see the ruins. The Incas who built Machu Picchu were great architects. My family and I climbed the steps all the way up to the Sun Gate. It was a steep climb. We stopped to rest a few times because I was extremely tired. At the top, it was wonderful. We could see everything! I think my photos are fabulous. Tell me what you think.

---

19 **Write.** Write a blog entry about a family holiday or a special day. Describe your thoughts and feelings.

20 **Work in a group.** Share your writing. Listen and make notes.

NATIONAL GEOGRAPHIC

Mission

Value your cultural traditions.

- Work with a friend. What local culture and traditions are in danger?

- Why should we keep our culture and traditions alive? List some ideas in the box.

So we all remember our history.

- Work in a group. Share your ideas. Are they the same or different? Which ideas does everyone like best?

'I'm committed to protecting the cultures of the world in the hope that the wisdom of their elders is remembered.'

Elizabeth Kapu'uwailani Lindsey
Filmmaker/Anthropologist
National Geographic Fellow

21 **Make a time capsule of things that show your culture.**

1. Work in small groups.

2. Talk about things that show your culture.

3. Choose the best things to include.

4. Put the objects in your time capsule.

Now I can ...

○ talk about why it's good to hold on to traditions.

○ explain how the past makes me who I am.

○ write a blog.

We put in a smartphone as something new. But we also put in my grandmother's embroidered handkerchief because it's old and traditional.

Amazing Plants!

In this unit, I will ...
- talk about how plants adapt.
- discuss the importance of plants.
- compare plants.
- write a descriptive paragraph.

Tick T for *True* or F for *False*.

1. These flowers are sculptures.   (T) (F)

2. The flowers are wet.   (T) (F)

3. These flowers eat insects.   (T) (F)

Australian sundew

Have you ever heard of a flower that smells like rotting meat to **attract** insects? Have you ever seen a plant close its **leaves** over an insect? Can plants really do these things? Let's learn more about the **behaviour** of plants.

Pitcher plant

Plants need **light**, air, water and nutrients to live. **Roots** absorb the nutrients that are in the **ground** and water. Tiny organisms called **bacteria** turn these nutrients into food that the plant can use. But some places don't have a lot of these nutrients. So, some plants **adapt**. They follow a different plan for **survival**. Their **strategy** is to eat insects!

Stink lily, Panama

Venus flytrap, Southern Brazil

a leaf

a stem

The stink lily gets its name from its smell. The flower **smells** like rotting meat. The smell attracts flies to the plant – and then **tricks** them! When a fly crawls on the flower, pollen sticks to the fly. Then, the fly takes the pollen and leaves it on the next plant it visits. That's how the stink lily makes new plants.

The Venus flytrap attracts insects with a sweet odour. When an insect lands on an open leaf, the leaf closes and **traps** the insect. Then the plant slowly **digests** the insect over a period of eight to ten days.

3 **Work with a friend.** What did you learn? Ask and answer.

How do plants adapt to survive?

Some plants trap insects.

91

4 **Listen, read and sing.** TR: B4

Plants Are All Around

Leaf and stem and flower and root!
The sweet, delicious smell of fruit
is here and there and everywhere!
Plants are all around.

Plants are growing
up and down.
Air is flowing
all around.

Plants come in every shape and size.
Their bright colours attract the eyes
of bees and butterflies.

Big and small,
plants survive it all.

CHORUS

Some plants play tricks with our eyes.
They're made to give us a surprise.
A plant is designed to survive.
To make new seeds, to grow and thrive.

Some of the oldest plants on Earth
are trees on mountains high,
drinking in the light,
reaching up into the sky.

Leaf and stem and flower and root!
The sweet, delicious smell of fruit
is here and there and everywhere!
Plants are all around.

5 **Work with a friend.** Ask and answer.

1. Which plants do you like best?

2. Do you eat them?

3. What makes them special to you?

Passionflower

Insects **are attracted** to the plant's sweet smell.
The seeds **are carried** away by birds.

How **is** the insect **trapped**?
The fly **is caught** inside the closing leaves.

6 Read and complete the sentences.

1. Plant food _____is made_____ (make) by bacteria.

2. Pollen _____ (take) to other plants by insects.

3. The seeds _____ (carry) by birds.

4. Plants that eat insects _____ (find) in the

   rainforest.

5. Many new plants _____ (discover) every year.

7 Read. Underline the correct word.

Socotra **is located** / **is called** in the Indian Ocean. Many strange trees
are found / **are needed** here. One famous tree **is attracted** / **is called**
the dragon blood tree. It **is used** / **is found** to make paint and medicine.
The desert rose **is used** / **is found** in the desert in Socotra. It has beautiful
pink flowers. It **is shaped** / **is found** like an elephant's foot!

Dragon blood trees

8 **Read and write.** Rewrite the sentences.

1. Plants need nutrients for survival.

Nutrients are needed by plants for survival.

2. Birds eat the fruit.

_____

3. The plant attracts insects.

_____

4. The smell of the stink lily tricks the flies.

_____

5. The pitcher plant traps and digests insects.

_____

9 **Work with a friend.** How many sentences can you make? Take turns.

snacks	need	children
flowers	find	plants
insects	eat	flowers

Flowers are eaten by plants.

That's not true!

95

10 **Listen and repeat.** Then, read and write. TR: B6

a rose

a thorn

a petal

a daisy

a vine

1. The outer part of a flower is called a _____petal_____.

2. A climbing _____ holds onto things as it grows.

3. Be careful! That _____ is sharp.

4. The class gave the teacher a red _____.

5. Is that flower a white _____?

11 **Work with a friend.** Give a clue. Listen and stick. Take turns.

That's a pretty white flower!

It's a daisy!

1   2   3   4   5

I don't want a plant **that** smells like rotting meat!
I like plants **that** trick and trap insects.

12 **Read and write.**

sunflower / stem   daisy / petals   garden / flowers   rainforest / vines
rose / thorns   tree / leaves   Venus flytrap / insects

1. A sunflower is a plant that's got a long stem.
   _____

2. _____

3. _____

4. _____

5. _____

6. _____

7. _____

13 **Play a game. Work in groups of three.** Choose a page in this book. Describe an object. The group guesses what it is. The winner picks another page.

Go to page 59. This is something that flies through space.

It's a rocket.

No. Try again.

It's a comet!

Is That a *Plant?*

The flower of the *Hydnora africana* looks like a hungry mouth! Inside is white material that smells horrible. Insects are attracted to the smell. The insect is trapped inside the flower by stiff hairs. The insect eats the white material to survive. Pollen sticks to the insect. A few days later, the flower opens and the insect is free. Then it takes the pollen to another flower. The flower has done its job!

The white baneberry is also called 'doll's eyes'. Its fruit looks like eyes on blood-red stems! It is round and white and has a black dot. Birds eat the fruit and spread the seeds. That's how the doll's eyes makes other plants. The fruit does not hurt the birds, but it's poisonous to people! If people touch any part of the plant, they will get blisters! Eating the fruit can stop a person's heart.

The flower of the *Rafflesia arnoldii* is the largest of any plant! It can grow to be 1 metre (3 feet) across and can weigh 11 kilos (24 pounds). The flower looks scary. Things that look like big thorns grow out of its centre. And what is worse, it smells like rotting meat – just like the stink lily! But this plant doesn't eat insects. The odour attracts insects that carry its pollen to other plants. This big flower only blooms for five days. Because there are fewer and fewer of these plants, they may become extinct.

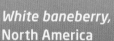

White baneberry, North America

	Hydnora africana	*Rafflesia arnoldii*	White baneberry
Leaves and stems	no	no	yes
Poisonous	no	no	yes
Horrible smell	yes	yes	no
Flower size	6 cm. (2.36 in.)	1 m. (3.28 ft.)	10 cm. (3.93 in.)
Fruit	yes	yes	yes

15 **Tick T for _True_ or F for _False_.**

1. The white baneberry has a horrible smell that attracts insects. Ⓣ Ⓕ

2. The fruit of the _Hydnora africana_ is very poisonous. Ⓣ Ⓕ

3. The _Rafflesia arnoldii_ does not have any leaves or stems. Ⓣ Ⓕ

4. Birds avoid the white baneberry. Ⓣ Ⓕ

5. The _Rafflesia arnoldii_ eats the insects that walk on it. Ⓣ Ⓕ

6. When the _Hydnora africana_ traps an insect, it lets it go in a few days. Ⓣ Ⓕ

16 **Work with a friend.** Put the plants in order (1 = most favourite). Explain why.

Order	Plant	Why the plant is brilliant
	Hydnora africana	
	Rafflesia arnoldii	
	Rose	
	Venus flytrap	
	White baneberry	
	Your choice _____	

17 **Invent a brilliant plant. Draw it and explain what it does.** Work in a small group. Share your plant.

The _Welwitschia mirabilis_ can live without rain for years. Some have lived for 2,000 years!

99

Descriptive Paragraphs

A descriptive paragraph describes what you see, feel, taste and hear. You can organise your description of a person, place or thing in different ways. You can describe the big parts first and then the small parts. You can go from big to small, from top to bottom, from the inside to the outside and so on.

18 **Read.** Read about the sensitive plant. How does the writer describe it? How does the writer organise the description?

The sensitive plant

Did you know that some plants can move? The sensitive plant moves when you touch it. The stem has tiny white hairs, and it stands straight up. It grows to about 50 centimetres. It has lots of thin green leaves. Each thin leaf is made of lots of tiny parts. The parts are like tiny leaves. These tiny leaves grow on both sides of each leaf stem.

When you touch a leaf, the tiny leaves fold up. Two by two, starting from where you touch, they close up. The leaf stem hangs down, too. It looks like it is hiding and does not want you to touch it. After half an hour, the plant stands up – until you touch it again!

Sensitive plant

19 **Write.** Write about the plant you invented. Describe it. Organise your description. Is your plant amazing? Why, or why not? Explain.

20 **Work in a group.** Share your writing. Listen and make notes.

NATIONAL GEOGRAPHIC
Mission

Value plants.

- What plants are important in your community?

- Why are these plants important? How are they used?

- Work in a small group. Choose a plant. Discuss why it is important. Write your ideas in the box.

We eat this plant.

'On my first trip to the rainforest, I met a woman who was in terrible pain because no one in her village could remember which plant would cure her. I saw that knowledge was truly being lost, and in that moment I knew this was what I wanted to do with my life.'

Maria Fadiman, Ethnobotanist
Emerging Explorer

- Get together with another group. Share your ideas. Are they the same or different? Which idea does everyone like best?

Green tea

21 **Make a local plant guide.**

1. Work with a friend. Choose a local plant.

2. Research the plant. Collect or draw pictures.

3. Glue and label the pictures.

4. Describe the plant and how it is used.

The aloe vera plant's got thick, pointy leaves. It is used for sunburn.

Aloe Vera Plant

Aloe vera comes from Africa, but it grows in many places. Its leaves are thick and pointy. Aloe vera likes full sun. It is good for sunburn.

Now I can ...

- ○ talk about how plants adapt.
- ○ discuss the importance of plants.
- ○ compare plants.
- ○ write a descriptive paragraph.

Review

1 **Read.** Complete the paragraphs. Use words from the list.

adapt	embroidery	handmade	no one	tourists
anyone	extraterrestrial	hold on	strategy	trap
astronaut	galaxy	leaves	survival	weave

1. Do you think _____ is listening to us from outer space? _____ knows the answer to this question, but scientists are discussing the possibility of intelligent _____ life.

2. The Huichol people in Mexico create traditional art to help them _____ to their culture. Selling their _____ art to _____ helps the future of their community.

3. The resurrection fern has learnt to _____ to dry climates. When there isn't enough rain, it looks dead. But this is just a _____ for _____. The plant is alive! When it rains, the dry _____ turn green.

2 **Work with a friend.** Practise and perform a role play.

Student A:
You think there might be life on other planets.

Student B:
You don't believe there is life on other planets.

anyone	everyone	journey	no one	someone	universe
communicate	galaxy	may/might	planet	spacecraft	

I think there might be life on planets in other solar systems.

If you're right, why doesn't anyone from other planets communicate with us?

3 **Work with a friend.** Listen to true sentences. Then read the sentences below. Tick T for *True* or F for *False*. TR: B9

1. Traditions are passed down from one generation to the next. Ⓣ Ⓕ

2. Languages must be protected from dying out. Ⓣ Ⓕ

3. Some plants are trapped by flies. Ⓣ Ⓕ

4. Insect-eating plants are called *carnivorous*. Ⓣ Ⓕ

5. The possibility of human life has been debated by extraterrestrials for a long time. Ⓣ Ⓕ

4 **Work in small groups.**

1. Write eight definitions using the word *that* on strips of paper.
2. Cut the strips just before the word *that*.
3. Mix up the paper strips and swap your paper strips with another group.
4. Match the strips of paper and read the sentences aloud. The group with the most correct sentences wins.

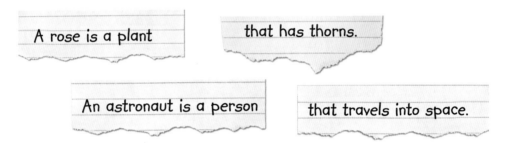

A rose is a plant | that has thorns.

An astronaut is a person | that travels into space.

5 **Write.** Choose four objects from the list. Write clues for your friend to guess.

comet	rocket	space station
jewellery	satellite	TV
pottery	sculpture	vine

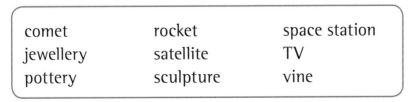

This is something that many women wear on their ears or around their neck.

Jewellery!

Let's Talk

Can I borrow your bike, please?

I will ...
- make an informal request.
- make an excuse.
- show understanding / accept 'no' for an answer.

---

1 **Listen and read.** TR: B10

Lucia: **Roberto, can I borrow** your bike this weekend, please?

Roberto: Er, **I'm really sorry**, but it's new. My dad won't let me lend it out.

Lucia: **That's OK. I understand.** Marcelo, **can you lend me** *your* bike?

Marcelo: **Yes, of course.** But please bring it back to me on Sunday, OK?

Can I borrow ..., please? **Can you lend me ..., please?** Is it OK if I use ...?	**I'm really sorry.** I'm sorry, but ... I can't. It isn't mine.	**That's OK. I understand.** Don't worry.
	Yes, of course. OK. Here you are! Yes, you can borrow _____. Of course. I can lend you _____. Of course.	Bring it back later, OK? Don't forget to bring it back, please.

2 **Work with a friend.** Use the table. Take turns to lend and borrow objects.

It could work.

I will ...
- make a suggestion.
- agree and disagree.
- respond.

3 **Listen and read.** TR: B11

Lin: **I think we should** interview a scientist for our project.

Cheng: **That's a good idea.**

Mei: **Yes, but** we haven't got time.

Jiang: **Actually, that could work.** My uncle is a scientist! I'll text him!

I think we should _____. I know what we should do! We should ... Why don't we ...? What if we ...?	**That's a good idea.** Why not? That could be good.	**Yes, but** _____. I don't think that'll work. I'm not sure.	**Actually, that could work.** That might work.
			In fact, I think _____. We could also _____.

4 **Listen.** You will hear two discussions. Does everyone agree at the end of the discussions? Circle the answer. TR: B12

1. Yes   No

2. Yes   No

5 **Work in a group.** Prepare and practise discussions. Choose one of the three situations given below.

1. Let's interview a famous person!

2. Why don't we do a report with a big map?

3. I think we should make a collage of volcanoes on the classroom wall.

107

Volcanoes

In this unit, I will ...
- discuss volcanoes.
- describe how a volcano erupts.
- make predictions.
- write a process paragraph.

Tick T for *True* or F for *False*.

1. Red-hot rocks are thrown into the air. (T) (F)

2. We can see the steam and smoke. (T) (F)

3. The lava glows in the dark. (T) (F)

Stromboli volcano, Sicily, Italy

1 **Listen and read.** TR: B13

2 **Listen and repeat.** TR: B14

Go for a walk on a sunny day. The earth seems **calm** under your feet. But **deep** down, it isn't. Under the earth's crust, it is so hot that rock **melts**. This **molten rock** is called magma.

In some places, there are deep **cracks** in the **surface** of the earth. These cracks let magma come to the surface. The magma pushes up the earth's crust. It **creates** a living mountain, called a **volcano**!

A volcano **erupts** when magma **explodes** onto the surface. The flow of this rock is called lava. The lava is thrown into the air and oozes down the volcano. The **heat** of the lava burns everything it touches.

The blast of an eruption throws **steam** into the air. The steam is created from water **inside** the earth. The blast also sends **gases** high into the sky. They make breathing difficult. A volcanic eruption can fill the sky with **ash**. Big eruptions **cover** the land with a **thick** layer of ash.

a volcano

surface   inside

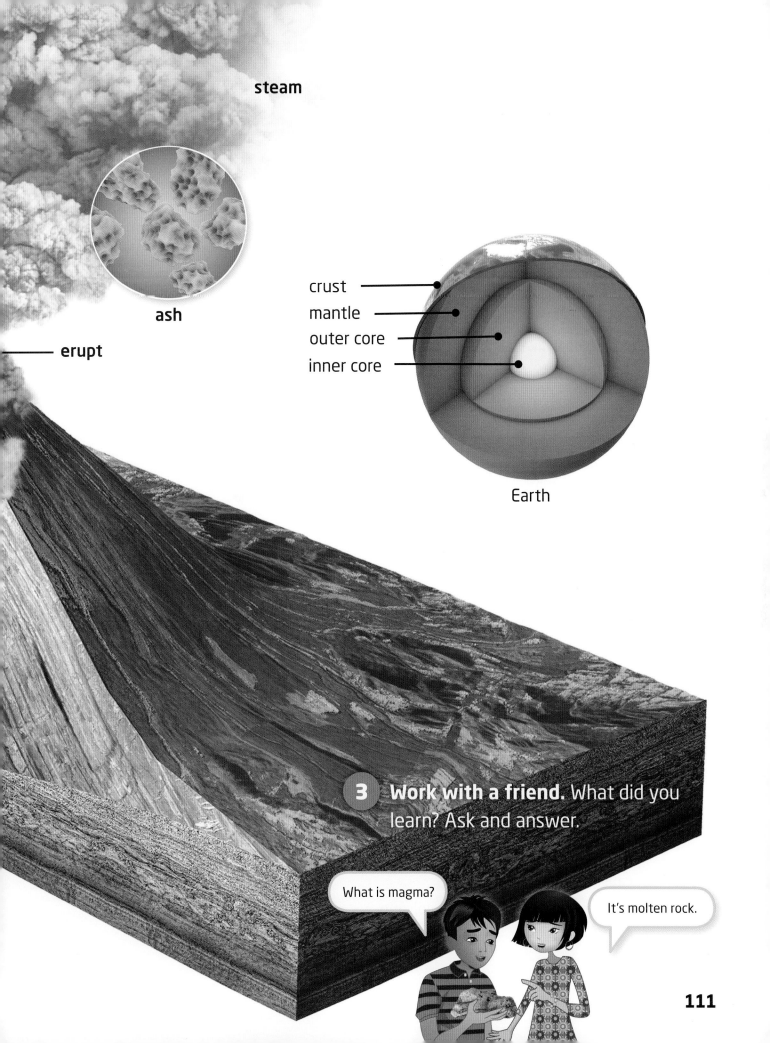

steam

ash

erupt

crust
mantle
outer core
inner core

Earth

3 **Work with a friend.** What did you learn? Ask and answer.

What is magma?

It's molten rock.

4 **Listen, read and sing.** TR: B15

Volcanoes Are a Lot Like Me

Volcanoes are a lot like me.
Some are awake and full of energy.
Other volcanoes are sleeping.
Yes, volcanoes are a lot like me!

When I get really silly,
and I'm bursting with energy.
If it's got nowhere to go,
sometimes I think I will explode!

Deep inside a volcano,
heat and gas are building up.
If they've got nowhere to go,
the volcano will erupt!

CHORUS

If a volcano is dormant,
it's really just asleep.
A dormant volcano will sleep for centuries.

If a volcano is active,
it's wide awake.
When it's awake, it's just like me.
It's ready to burn off some energy!

CHORUS

5 **Work with a friend.** Discuss.

1. Sometimes I'm like an active volcano because ...

2. Sometimes I'm like a dormant volcano because ...

Mount St Helens, Washington, USA

GRAMMAR TR: B16

If the lava **touches** the trees, it **will** burn them.
If rain **hits** the lava, it'**ll** turn into steam.

I **will go** to a safe place **if** the volcano **erupts**.
The plants **will burn if** hot ash **covers** them.

6 **Read.** Write sentences.

1. I go to Hawaii / I see volcanoes

If I go to Hawaii, I will see volcanoes.

2. I run away / volcano erupts

_____

3. ash covers the grass / the grass die

_____

4. lava reaches the sea / it turn into steam

_____

5. no aeroplanes fly / ash fills the sky

_____

Kilauea, Hawaii, USA

7 **Write four sentence halves beginning with If.** Work in pairs. Take turns. Complete each other's sentences.

8 **Work in small groups.** Build each new sentence onto the sentence before.

9 **Listen and repeat.** Then, read and write. TR: B17

dormant

cone

active

crater

extinct

1. If a volcano is erupting, then it is _____ active _____.

2. If a volcano is not erupting, but might erupt in the future, it is

_____.

3. If a volcano has not erupted in thousands of years and will

not erupt in the future, it is _____.

4. The hole left at the top of a volcano that has erupted is called a

_____.

5. The sides of a volcano form the _____ at the top.

10 **Listen and stick.** Work with a friend. Discuss. TR: B18

How do you know if a volcano is extinct?

You have to read about it before climbing it!

1   2   3   4   5

Because of the ash, the animals could not breathe.
The trees died **because of** the heat from the lava.

11 **Read and write.**

1. rocks flew into the sky / the eruption

The rocks flew into the sky because of the eruption.

2. the heat / no one could get close to the crater

_____

3. it was difficult to see / the ash

_____

4. we saw white clouds in the sky / the steam

_____

5. the blast / the eruption could be heard from far away

_____

12 **Play a game.** Play with a friend. Cut out the cards on page 169 and put them face down in a pile. Choose a card and start a sentence. Take turns. Complete your friend's sentences.

Because of the ash ...

we couldn't play outside.

117

Active Volcanoes

There are active volcanoes all over the world. Some erupt quite often, sending hot lava down their slopes. People often live near these volcanoes. Because of the ash, the land is good for farming.

The longest-erupting volcano is Mount Etna, in Sicily. It has been active for 3,500 years. Mount Etna erupts very often. It has destroyed lots of towns. People have tried to change the lava flow. They've built walls made of earth and used explosives. Some towns have avoided destruction. Successful evacuation plans have kept people safe.

Five volcanoes created the island of Hawaii. Mauna Loa is the largest volcano in the world. Kīlauea is one of the most active. In fact, it almost never stops erupting. The fumes from this great volcano are also a problem for local people.

The volcano Nyamuragira, in Africa, erupts about every two years. It also has big lava flows. It creates smaller volcanoes on its sides. At one time, the volcano had a crater with a lake of lava in it. Then, in 1938, there was an eruption that opened up one side of the volcano. Because of the eruption, the lava lake flowed out of the crater. People do not live near this volcano.

Popocatépetl is about 70 kilometres from Mexico City. An eruption in 2000 made 50,000 people leave their homes. In 2012, Popocatépetl covered cars and streets with ash. Every March, people honour the volcano by offering it food and music.

Weird but true

The largest known volcano is on Mars. It is about 22,000 m. tall and 700 km. across!

Mauna Ulu, Hawaii, USA

14 Read and circle the letter.

1. This volcano had a lake of lava in its crater.

   a. Mount Etna   b. Nyamuragira   c. Stromboli

2. This is the largest volcano on the island of Hawaii.

   a. Mauna Loa   b. Kīlauea   c. Popocatépetl

3. This volcano's eruption caused the evacuation of 50,000 people.

   a. Nyamuragira   b. Popocatépetl   c. Puychue

4. This is the longest-erupting volcano.

   a. Kīlauea   b. Vesuvius   c. Mount Etna

15 Where are these volcanoes? Work with a friend.

Kīlauea

Mount Etna

Nyamuragira

Mauna Loa

Popocatépetl

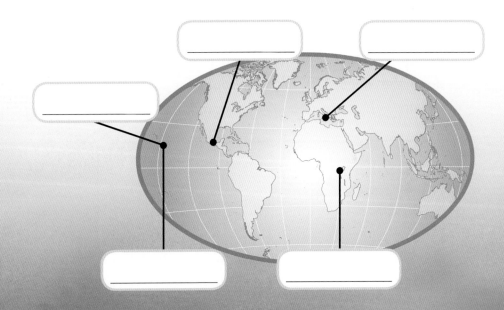

16 Work with a friend. Read the text again. Talk about two volcanoes. Take turns. Make notes.

Name of volcano	Notes
1	
2	

Process Paragraphs

A process paragraph explains what happens in a sequence. It follow a series of actions from beginning to end. Use words such as *first, then, next, after, when, while, at the same time, now, before, as long as* and *finally*. These words show the order in which actions, or stages, occur.

17 **Read.** Read the paragraphs about the stages of a volcanic eruption. How does the writer show the sequence of events? Underline the words.

How volcanoes erupt

First, the heat deep inside the earth melts the rocks. Next, the trapped magma pushes on the top and along the walls of the volcano. At the same time, trapped gases push on the cone. There is nowhere for it to escape. When the pushing gets very strong, the walls become weak. After some time, the top of the volcano blasts away.

Finally, the magma and gases explode out of the top. Gases and steam come out. The volcano throws ash high into the air. Lava flows down the sides. The volcano erupts for as long as the magma pushes upwards. If there is a lot of magma, it can erupt for a long time.

18 **Write.** Describe a process that you know. Explain the steps from beginning to end.

19 **Work in a small group.** Share your writing.

NATIONAL GEOGRAPHIC

Mission

Help in a disaster.

- We hear about disasters all over the world. Work in a group. What can you do to help in a disaster?

- How can you get the community involved? Who can donate money or supplies? How could you send them to the disaster area? Write your ideas in the box.

'Crisis mapping can pinpoint urgent needs instantly, saving time and lives,'

Patrick Meier, Crisis Mapper
Emerging Explorer

We can raise some money.

- Work with another group. Share your ideas. Are they the same or different? Which idea does everyone like best?

Mount Snowdon, Wales, UK

20 Make a model of an erupting volcano.

1. Get a cardboard tube about 4 cm. wide and 20 cm. long.

2. Cover the bottom of the tube with clay. Stick the tube onto cardboard.

3. Make balls of newspaper. Stick them to the tube to make a cone.

4. Cover the cone with aluminium foil. Glue sand onto it.

5. Fill half of the tube with baking soda.

6. Add red food colouring to vinegar. Pour it into the tube and watch it erupt!

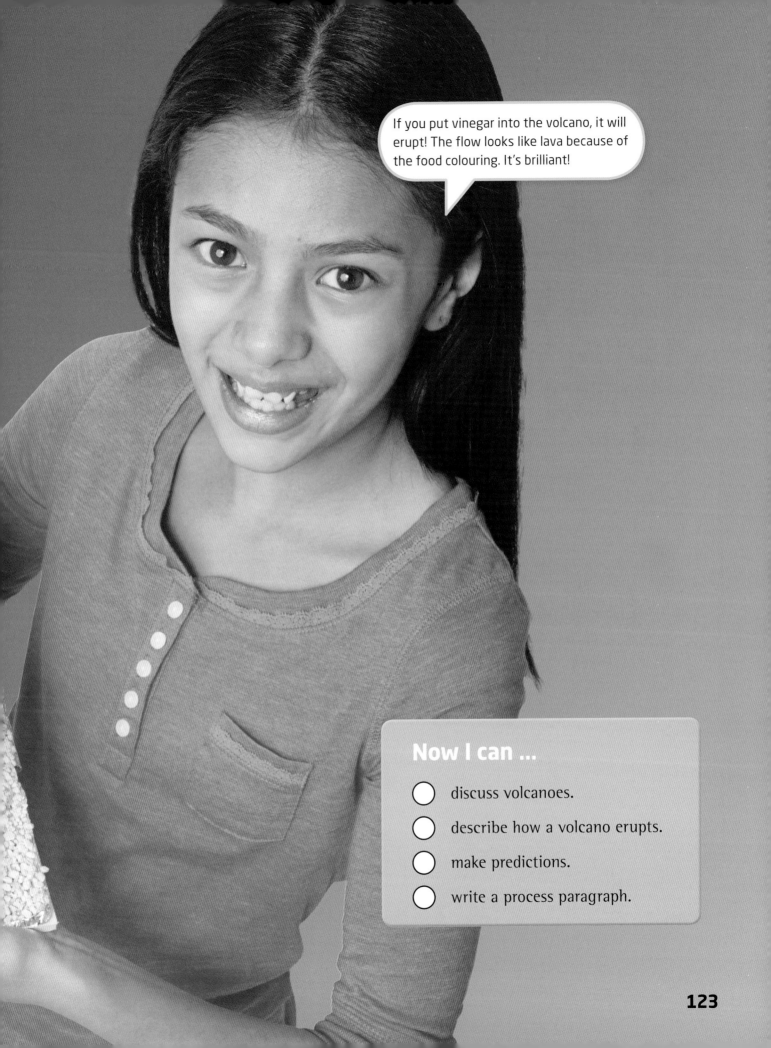

If you put vinegar into the volcano, it will erupt! The flow looks like lava because of the food colouring. It's brilliant!

Now I can ...

- ◯ discuss volcanoes.
- ◯ describe how a volcano erupts.
- ◯ make predictions.
- ◯ write a process paragraph.

Reduce, Reuse, Recycle

In this unit, I will ...
- discuss the importance of reducing, reusing and recycling.
- discuss art made from recycled materials.
- talk about what I can do to help the environment.
- write a biographical paragraph.

Tick T for *True* or F for *False*.

1. There are about one hundred sculptures.　Ⓣ Ⓕ

2. Each sculpture is a bit different.　Ⓣ Ⓕ

3. The sculptures are made from rubbish.　Ⓣ Ⓕ

4. This is a landfill site.　Ⓣ Ⓕ

HA Schult's *Trash People*,
Barcelona, Spain

Every day we create **rubbish**. Where does it go? Some of it is buried in **landfill sites**. Yuck! There has to be a better way! There is! You can choose a way of life that works with the **environment**. You can **save** instead of **throw away**. You can make **energy-efficient** choices!

The three Rs of the environment are *reduce*, *reuse* and *recycle*. We all know about recycling. **Man-made** things are crushed and melted down. They are then made into new things. The best Rs are to reduce and reuse. Reduce by choosing to use less energy. Reuse by finding new uses for **rubbish**.

Choosing **natural** materials is better for the environment. Things made from natural materials are amazing! When they are used up, just like other rubbish, they go into the landfill site, too. But they break down more quickly. And, natural things can be grown again. They're **renewable**!

Can we **design** things to reduce, reuse and recycle? Yes! We can **build** houses that are energy-efficient. We can create art with natural things, or reused things. The possibilities are endless!

3 **Work with a friend.** What did you learn? Ask and answer.

How can I save energy?

Turn off the lights when you aren't using them.

That's right! Reduce.

4 **Listen, read and sing.** TR: B23

The Three Rs

When you're walking to the rubbish bin
with some rubbish in your hand,
you might want to stop and think again.
Can this be reused or given away?
Let's start looking after our world today!

Reduce. Reuse. Recycle.
Do it every day.
Don't throw everything away
when clearly there's another way.

Reduce. Reuse. Recycle.
Help to keep our world clean.
Do your part every day
to make our world green!

Recycling is easy when you know what to do.
Glass? Paper? Metal?
These things can be reused
again, and again and again!

CHORUS

Compost your uneaten food.
Composting isn't hard to do.
Natural things can be reused
when they get a helping hand from you!

Reduce. Reuse. Recycle.
Do it every day.
Don't throw everything away
when clearly there's another way.

Reduce. Reuse. Recycle.
Help to keep our world clean.
Reduce. Reuse. Recycle.
Help make our world green!

5 **Work with a friend.** Ask and answer.

How do you reduce, reuse or recycle?

- glass
- paper
- metal

128

Natural things **can be grown** again.   Aluminium cans **must be melted** to be recycled.
Many things **can be made** into art.   Some plastics **may be put** in recycling containers.

6 **Read.** Complete the sentences. Use the words in the list.

> reused   made   coloured   thrown away   built   saved   designed

1. Clothes (can / colour) _____*can be coloured*_____ with natural dyes.

2. Save the bricks that (can / reuse) _____, and the broken

   ones (can / throw away) _____.

3. Energy (may / save) _____ by making good choices.

4. Fleece jumpers (can / make) _____ from recycled

   water bottles.

5. Future cars (must / design) _____ to run on electricity.

6. A house (can / build) _____ with recycled materials.

7 **What things can be done to reduce, reuse and recycle?** Use the words in the list. Write sentences.

'green' shopping bags	repair
magazine	reuse
water	recycle
energy-efficient houses	save
a tap with a leak	design

1. _Water can be saved._ _____

2. _____

3. _____

4. _____

5. _____

8 **Work with a friend.** Read one of your sentences. Your friend makes a sentence using the same verb. Take turns.

Water can be saved.

Electricity can be saved, too.

9 **Listen and repeat.**
Then, read and write. TR: B25

chemicals

cardboard

metal

glass

tools

1. It is clear or coloured. It can be melted down and reused. It is used to make bottles and windows. _____glass_____

2. It is made from paper. It is used to make shoe boxes. It is soft when wet.

   _____

3. They are used to clean things. They can hurt your skin. Don't drink them!

   _____

4. There are many kinds, and they have different uses. They help us to do things that we can't do with only our hands. _____

5. This is used to make aluminium cans and cars. It is used to make things that must be strong. _____

10 **Listen and stick.** TR: B26

1	2	3	4	5

When we recycle rubbish, we save on materials and energy.
An artist's work may surprise us **when we first see it**.

11 **Read and write.** How do you and your friends help
the environment? Use the words in the box.

bike   light   paper   plastic bottle   shopping bag   rubbish   water

1. When _____we leave the house_____ , _____we turn off the lights_____ .

2. _____ when _____ .

3. When _____ , _____ .

4. When _____ , _____ .

5. _____ when _____ .

12 **Play a game.** Cut out the spinner on page 171. Work in a small
group. Make sentences. Take turns.

I reuse a shopping bag
when I go shopping.

Found Art

We often think of reusing and recycling as something we just have to do. But some people see it as a chance to create. Any object can be reused to make something amazing. Reusing is more than a way to save – it can help us think about things in new and different ways.

Using found objects to make art is not new. *Found art* became popular in the 1900s. Found art made people think about the things around them in a different way. Many things could be made into art!

Today, many artists still create art from things they find. Sometimes they use things as they find them, and other times they make changes to the things they find. Sometimes they use rubbish. The artists put it all together to express their thoughts. We can enjoy their creativity and be amazed at the artists' skill. We can also be surprised by our feelings. Often, we can just appreciate the beauty or the humour. All these things make found art valuable in our lives.

Weird but true

Recycling old aluminium cans into new ones uses 95% less energy than making new cans.

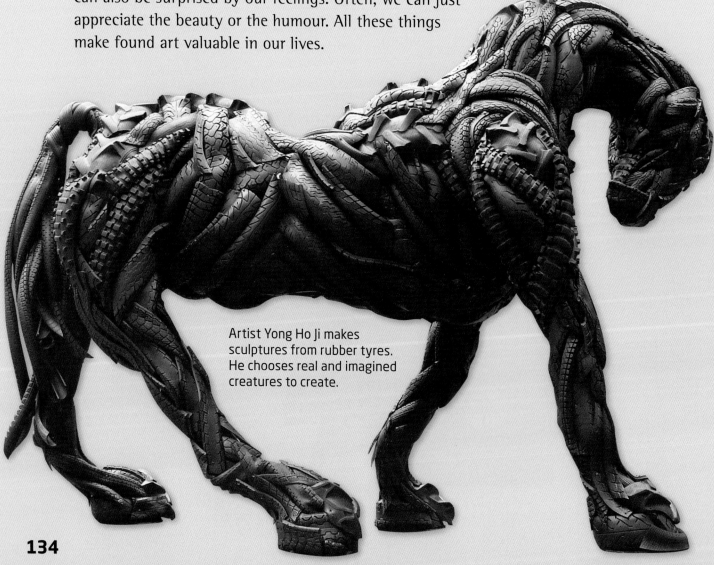

Artist Yong Ho Ji makes sculptures from rubber tyres. He chooses real and imagined creatures to create.

14 **Tick T for *True* or F for *False*.**

1. Using old objects to make art is a way to reuse rubbish. (T) (F)

2. Found art always uses rubbish. (T) (F)

3. Art made from rubbish is valuable because it makes us think in new ways. (T) (F)

4. Found art started in the 1850s. (T) (F)

5. Yong Ho Ji makes sculptures from rubber tyres. (T) (F)

15 **Label.** Use these words.

fork

key

pencil sharpener

spoon

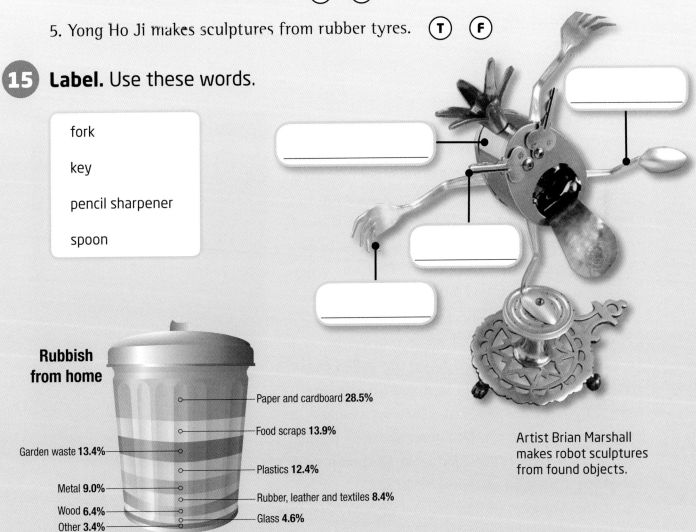

Rubbish from home

Paper and cardboard **28.5%**

Food scraps **13.9%**

Garden waste **13.4%**

Plastics **12.4%**

Metal **9.0%**

Rubber, leather and textiles **8.4%**

Wood **6.4%**

Glass **4.6%**

Other **3.4%**

Artist Brian Marshall makes robot sculptures from found objects.

16 **Vote on the most creative work of art.** Work in a group. Look at these photos and the photo on pages 124 and 125. Discuss the art. Which do you like best? Explain why. Does your group agree?

17 **Make more rubbish art.** Work with a friend. Discuss creating rubbish art. What would you make and what materials would you use?

135

Biographical Paragraphs

A biographical paragraph tells about the life and work of a person. You can include key dates, such as date of birth, important events and interesting facts about the person's life. You should also explain why this person is, or was, important. Use expressions such as *one of the most famous* and *the first.*

18 **Read.** Read about Marcel Duchamp. Find out facts about his life. Identify reasons why he was considered important.

Marcel Duchamp

Marcel Duchamp was born in France in 1887. He was one of the most important modern artists of the 1900s. His first famous works were abstract paintings. These paintings showed a general idea of something, not just objects in the way people usually see them. This was a new way of creating art, and lots of people did not understand it. It was shocking to many people.

Duchamp was the first modern artist to create art from things he found. He called these objects 'readymades'. His first readymade was the 'Bicycle Wheel'. At first, other artists said this work was not art. Duchamp shocked people! Later on, artists understood what Duchamp was creating. A version of this work of art is at the Museum of Modern Art in New York City.

Bicycle Wheel by Marcel Duchamp, 1913

19 **Write.** Write about an important or interesting person. Include important details and dates from the person's life. Explain why he or she is important.

20 **Work in a small group.** Share your writing.

NATIONAL GEOGRAPHIC
Mission

Help reduce our human footprint.

- What can your community do to reduce, reuse and recycle?

- Think of ways your community can reduce waste. Think of ways it can reuse and recycle.

- Work in a group. Discuss ideas for the community. Write your ideas in the box.

'People have created the problem, so it's critical to get the public excited and eager to participate in a solution.'

Alexandra Cousteau
Water Advocate and
Environmental Filmmaker
Emerging Explorer

We can recycle waste paper.

- Share your ideas with another group. Are they the same or different? Decide which ideas everyone likes best.

Earth at night

21 Make art from things you throw away.

1. Work in a small group. Collect different types of recycling.

2. Look at your collected recycling and decide what to make.

3. Make your work of art.

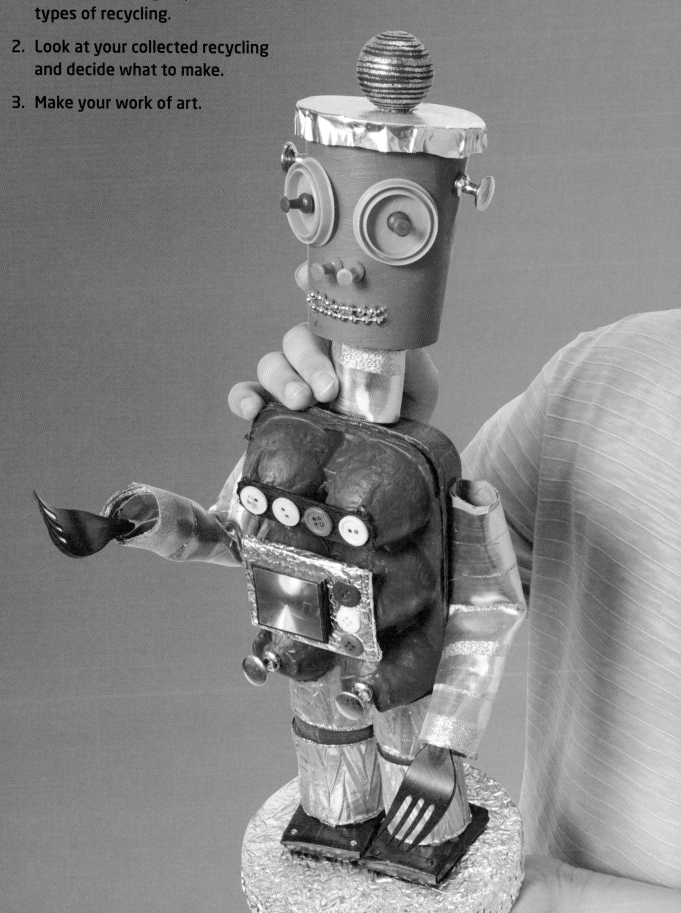

We made a robot sculpture. Our sculpture is made from recycled cardboard and reused plastic utensils and ornaments. Your recycling can be made into art, too!

Now I can ...

- ⃝ discuss the importance of reducing, reusing and recycling.

- ⃝ discuss art made from recycled materials.

- ⃝ talk about what I can do to help the environment.

- ⃝ write a biographical paragraph.

Wonderful Holidays!

In this unit, I will ...
- talk about different holiday destinations.
- talk about what I would do in different situations.
- express preferences.
- write a review.

Look and circle the correct letter.

1. What are the people doing?

   a. playing in a pool

   b. sliding down a water slide

2. Where are they?

   a. at a water park

   b. at a river

Water park, Beijing, China

1 Listen and read.

2 Listen and repeat.

Do you like holidays with lots of people and noise? Or places that are quiet with no people nearby? Let's find out about some wonderful holidays!

The whole family enjoys **camping** together. Bring a **tent** and sleep outside. If you **climb** a very big mountain, you have to take a **guide** to help you to find the way.

Do you like history? Go and see the **ruins** of an old city. If you like the modern world, go on a **tour** of a city! But if you like learning about how to protect the natural world, then an ecotour is for you!

Do you like animals and plants? Go on a **photo safari** and take pictures of **wildlife**. Stay safe in a vehicle when there are dangerous wild animals.

Santa Cruz, Peru

142

A resort is a good place to **relax** and have fun on your holiday. Stay the night at a big **hotel**. Go to the **beach** to sit in the sun and swim. Put sunblock on so that your skin doesn't burn!

Theme parks are full of people having fun! Buy a **ticket** for an exciting ride, and hear people scream. If the theme park is *Dreamworld*, then get ready to enter a world of fantasy! If the theme park is also a **water park**, get ready to get wet!

camping

3 **Work with a friend.** What did you learn? Ask and answer.

What would you like to do on holiday?

I'd like to go camping!

143

4 **Listen, read and sing.** TR: B31

If I Went on Holiday

Let's go on holiday!
Let's go on a trip!

If we went on holiday,
we would go on a big, big ship
across the sea,
a long way away.

If I had my way,
I would go today!

Camping and hiking!
The beach and the sun!
If we went on holiday,
it would be so much fun!

If we went on a tour,
we would see wildlife.
I'd take lots of photos.
Wouldn't that be so nice?

CHORUS

I would like to stay at a hotel.
You'd like to relax.

Camping and hiking!
The beach and the sun!
If we went on holiday,
it would be so much fun!

If I weren't afraid of heights,
we could climb a mountain.
But I am! So let's go to the water park
and take pictures by the fountain.

CHORUS

5 **Work with a friend.** Plan a holiday.

1. Where do you want to go? Why?

2. What will you take with you?

3. What will you do there?

144

Moremi Game Reserve, Botswana

GRAMMAR TR: B32

If we **went** on a photo safari, I **would take** pictures of lions.
I'd go mountain climbing if I **weren't** afraid of heights.
He **wouldn't spend** all of his time in museums if he **didn't like** art.
If you **had** a lot of money, where **would** you **go** on holiday?

6 **Read and write.**

1. If I ___went___ (go) to Egypt, I ___would see___ (see) the Great Pyramid.

2. If we _____ (stay) at a hotel near the beach, we _____
(go swimming).

3. She _____ (go camping) if she _____ (have) a tent.

4. We _____ (learn) about the animals in this region if we
_____ (go on) an ecotour.

5. If the tour guide _____ (come) with us, she _____
(tell) us all about this place.

6. If he _____ (get) the train, he _____ (see) more
of the country.

Tourist train, Victoria, Australia

7 **Work with a friend.** Look at the pictures and make sentences. Take turns.

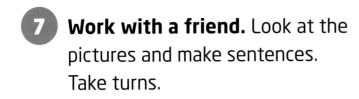

If I went to the beach, I would go snorkelling.

I would go surfing if I went to the beach.

8 Listen and repeat.
Then, read and write. TR: B33

a suitcase

sunglasses

a passport

souvenirs

an airport

1. When you travel to another country, you need a _____ passport _____ .

   It shows who you are and the country where you were born.

2. I always buy _____ when I'm on holiday. I like to look at

   them and remember the fun I had!

3. I don't like carrying a lot of things on holiday. I take a small

   _____ for my clothes.

4. If we arrived at the _____ late, we would miss our plane.

5. Has anyone seen my _____? The snow is so bright in

   the sunshine.

9 Listen and stick. Do you think they had a good holiday? Why? TR: B34

1   2   3   4   5

I **would rather** go on an ecotour than go to a theme park.
We**'d rather** go on a tour than stay at the hotel.
He**'d rather** not eat at that restaurant.

10 **Work with a friend.** Make sentences. Take turns.

1. live by the sea / in the mountains <u>I would rather live by the sea than live</u>

   <u>in the mountains.</u>

2. go camping / stay at a hotel _____

   _____

3. ride a bike on a dirt path / motorbike _____

   _____

4. walk in the forest / city _____

   _____

5. see wildlife on a photo safari / in the zoo _____

   _____

6. wear sunblock / get sunburnt _____

   _____

11 **Play a game.** Cut out the board and the pictures on page 173. Choose nine pictures and put them in the spaces. Do not show your pictures. Work with a friend. Take turns.

B2. Let's go to a water park.

I don't feel like it. I'd rather go for a walk.

12 Listen and read. TR: B36

Tree-house Holiday

Are you ready for a great eco-adventure? Have your holiday in a tree house! You can find them all over the world. Tree-house holidays are in destinations such as Brazil, Kenya, Belize and India. There's lots to do in nature!

In India, there are tree-house bedrooms from 10 to 25 metres (35 to 80 feet) up a tree. There's a bamboo lift to carry you up. It's powered by water! The electricity you use comes from the sun. And there are tracks to walk on and natural swimming pools to swim in. You can visit your neighbour by walking across a bridge made of rope!

You can stay in comfort at a tree house in Kenya. It has two floors, and the rooms have big beds. The windows have coloured glass and the bathrooms have showers. There's a small kitchen, too. The hotel serves food in your room! And if you get tired of living in nature, the city of Nairobi is about 30 minutes away.

In Belize, you can live with parrots under a Guanacaste tree that is about 30 metres (100 feet) tall. The parrots make good neighbours because they eat the insects! There are other birds, too – so it's a great place for birdwatching. A river runs around the tree house on three sides. The clear water is good for swimming!

The largest tree-house-holiday destination is in the Amazon, in Brazil. There are many tree houses, all connected by more than 8 kilometres (5 miles) of wooden bridges. You can walk through the trees at about 25 metres (65 feet) high and see the wildlife. Your neighbour might be a monkey!

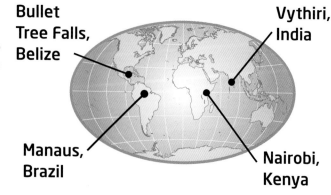

Bullet Tree Falls, Belize

Vythiri, India

Manaus, Brazil

Nairobi, Kenya

A company is planning future holidays on the moon! Some tourists have already visited the space station. But it's expensive!

13 **Where are these tree houses?** Read and write the location.

1. You can live with parrots in a tree house in _____.

2. You can have a holiday in comfort in a tree house in _____.

3. The largest tree-house-holiday destination is in _____.

4. A bamboo lift carries you to your tree house in _____.

14 **Work with a friend.** Compare destinations for a tree-house holiday. Your friend will listen and complete the first two rows. Then listen to your friend and fill in the last two rows.

Watching wildlife	
Living in comfort	
Walking on tree bridges	
Using power from nature	

15 **Places for a holiday.** Put the holidays in order of preference (1 = most favourite). Work with a friend. Compare and explain your choices.

Order	Holidays	Why you want to go there
	Ice hotel	
	Underwater hotel	
	Sports camp	
	Martial arts camp	
	Make-a-film camp	
	Astronaut camp	
	Tree house	

Reviews

To make your writing interesting, you can use different kinds of sentences. You can use short simple sentences to describe your ideas. Or you can combine your ideas into longer sentences. You can also use questions or exclamations.

16 **Read.** Read the ecotour review. Find sentences that describe only one idea, sentences that describe more than one idea, questions and exclamations.

Review of the Antigua ecotour

The ecotour in Antigua is a great choice for a holiday. The tour guide takes you to an island and shows you how to paddle a kayak. Then he leads you through a forest of mangroves. The guide knows a lot! He tells you about local fish and the history of the island. The forest is calm and beautiful. It's fun to paddle and not too tiring.

The best part of the tour is the hidden beaches. Why? You can see wildlife, such as pelicans, feeding their young. People wear snorkels when they swim over coral reefs. If you can't swim it's hard because the water can be rough. But it's worth the effort because there are amazing colourful fish to see. If you like water and nature, you should go!

coral reef

stingray

17 **Write.** Write a holiday review. Say what you liked and didn't like. Describe what you saw and did. Remember to use different types of sentences.

18 **Work in a small group.** Share your writing.

NATIONAL GEOGRAPHIC

Mission

Be a respectful tourist.

- Work with a friend. Is tourism always good for a place? How does it help and hurt local people?

- How can tourists show respect for the places they visit? Discuss things you can do, and things you shouldn't do. Make notes.

'To bridge cultures you must mix people together. Education and travel are the best teachers.'

Joseph Lekuton, Teacher
Emerging Explorer

You can learn about a country before your holiday.

- Share your ideas with a group. Are they the same or different? Decide which ideas everyone thinks are best.

Vancouver, British Columbia, Canada

19 Make a tourist brochure.

1. Work with a friend. Choose an interesting place in your country.

2. Find out about the place. What can you do there? What places can you visit?

3. Make a brochure with pictures and text.

Colonia
[del Sacramento],
Uruguay

Colonia was founded by the Portuguese in 1680 on the Río de la Plata.

The lighthouse was built in 1857 over the ruins of a convent. You can go to the top and see the views.

You can see Portuguese and Spanish architecture.

Map of Colonia del Sacramento

Río de la Plata

Museo Español

Plaza del Agosto

Plaza de Armas

Plaza Mayor

Bastión de San Miguel

Río de la Plata

There's a lot to do in Colonia. You should visit the lighthouse and the museums!

Now I can ...

- ○ talk about different holiday destinations.
- ○ talk about what I would do in different situations.
- ○ express preferences.
- ○ write a review.

Review

1 **Read.** Complete these sentences. Use each word only once. Then make similar sentences about yourself.

> because of   could   when   will   would

1. I couldn't go to the water park _____ because of _____ the rain.

2. If I have time, I _____ go to the new theme park.

3. A lot of rubbish _____ be made into art.

4. I _____ run away if a volcano erupted!

5. Some parts of our brain become active _____ we look at art.

2 **Work with a friend.** Talk about your dream holiday.

> if / will
> if / would
> would rather

> If my parents say yes, we will go on a photo safari!

> I would rather go to a water park!

> And if I didn't have to come to school, I would travel around the world for six months.

3 **Work with a friend.** Practise and perform a role play.

Student A:
You are a scientist who studies volcanoes. Answer the reporter's questions.

Student B:
You are a student interviewing the scientist for the school magazine. Ask questions.

> ash   dormant   erupt   extinct   heat   steam
> crater   environment   eruption   gas   lava   volcano

> Are dormant volcanoes dangerous?

> Yes, because sometimes they become active.

4

Work with a friend. Look at the photo. How can these things be reused?

1. Old cans can be _____.

2. _____.

3. _____.

4. _____.

5

Listen to the adverts. Tick the mini-holiday. TR: B37

	Photo safari	Ecotour
Visit exotic places near your home.	✓	
Get to know your own city.		
Bring a tent and a sleeping bag.		
Create art.		
Get up early on Sunday.		
Bring just a sleeping bag.		
Take pictures at the recycling centre.		

6

Work with a friend. Ask and answer.

1. What will you do this weekend if you have some spare time?

2. Which of the two weekend tours in Activity 5 would you rather do? Why?

3. If you could travel for six months, where would you go?

7

Work in small groups. Create a brochure for a weekend trip near your city.

camping	guide	rubbish	relax	suitcase	tent	ticket
environment	walk	natural	ruins	sunglasses	theme park	tour

157

Let's Talk

Definitely not!

I will ...
• agree and disagree.
• discuss possibilities.
• ask for opinions.

1 **Listen and read.** TR: B38

Maria: Are there any good films on tonight, Carla?

Carla: Well, there's a comedy. **What do you think?**

Ivana: **Definitely not!** Comedies are silly. **What else is there?**

Carla: Er, there's an action film. What do you think?

Ivana: Yes! Action films are the best!

Carla: **I suppose so.** But sometimes they're too violent.

Maria: **Exactly!** Isn't there anything else?

What do you think? How about _____?	Definitely not! Exactly! Yes, I agree. Definitely!	What else is there? Is(n't) there anything else? Anything else? Have you got any other ideas?	I suppose so. Maybe. Possibly.

2 **Work in groups of three.** Use the table. Discuss what to do this weekend.

Our presentation is about ...

I will ...
• introduce us.
• explain what our presentation is about.
• check with the audience.
• get started.

3 **Listen and read.** TR: B39

Gaby:	**Hello everyone. I'm Gaby** and **this is Berto**.
Berto:	**Our presentation is about** holidays.
Gaby:	**Today we're going to show you** our holiday brochure.
Berto:	**Our talk's got two parts.** So **I'll start** and then Gaby **will continue**.
Gaby:	**Can everyone see?**
Students:	Yes!
Berto:	Great. **Let's start.**

Hello (everyone). Good morning. Good afternoon, everyone.	I'm _____. This is _____. My name is _____. I'd like to present _____.	Our presentation/ project is about ... Our talk compares _____ with _____. Today we're going to (show you / present) _____. Our talk's got two parts.	Can everyone see/hear? Can you all see/hear?	Let's start. Let's get started. I'll start/ begin. _____ will continue.

4 **Listen.** Circle the object that students present in each discussion. TR: B40

1. Mia and Ivan are presenting   a. a brochure.   b. an invention.   c. a poster.

2. Sonia and Juan are presenting   a. a brochure.   b. an invention.   c. a poster.

5 **Work in pairs.** Prepare and practise presentations.

1. Show the class a brochure you made for your project.

2. Present an invention you created.

3. Show the class a poster you made.

Irregular Verbs

Infinitive	Past simple	Past participle	Infinitive	Past simple	Past participle
be	was/were	been	lie	lay	lain
beat	beat	beaten	light	lit	lit
become	became	become	lose	lost	lost
begin	began	begun	make	made	made
bend	bent	bent	meet	met	met
bite	bit	bitten	pay	paid	paid
bleed	bled	bled	put	put	put
blow	blew	blown	read	read	read
break	broke	broken	ride	rode	ridden
bring	brought	brought	ring	rang	rung
build	built	built	rise	rose	risen
buy	bought	bought	run	ran	run
catch	caught	caught	say	said	said
choose	chose	chosen	see	saw	seen
come	came	come	sell	sold	sold
cost	cost	cost	send	sent	sent
cut	cut	cut	set	set	set
dig	dug	dug	sew	sewed	sewn
do	did	done	shake	shook	shaken
draw	drew	drawn	shine	shone	shone
drink	drank	drunk	show	showed	shown
drive	drove	driven	shut	shut	shut
eat	ate	eaten	sing	sang	sung
fall	fell	fallen	sink	sank	sunk
feed	fed	fed	sit	sat	sat
feel	felt	felt	sleep	slept	slept
fight	fought	fought	slide	slid	slid
find	found	found	speak	spoke	spoken
fly	flew	flown	spend	spent	spent
forget	forgot	forgotten	spin	spun	spun
forgive	forgave	forgiven	stand	stood	stood
freeze	froze	frozen	steal	stole	stolen
get	got	got	stick	stuck	stuck
give	gave	given	sting	stung	stung
go	went	gone	smell	smelt	smelt
grow	grew	grown	sweep	swept	swept
hang	hung	hung	swim	swam	swum
have	had	had	swing	swung	swung
hear	heard	heard	take	took	taken
hide	hid	hidden	teach	taught	taught
hit	hit	hit	tear	tore	torn
hold	held	held	tell	told	told
hurt	hurt	hurt	think	thought	thought
keep	kept	kept	throw	threw	thrown
know	knew	known	understand	understood	understood
learn	learnt	learnt	wake up	woke up	woken up
leave	left	left	wear	wore	worn
lend	lent	lent	win	won	won
let	let	let	write	wrote	written

isn't it?	haven't they?	aren't they?	have they?
don't they?	do they?	doesn't it?	does it?
were they?	weren't they?	did it?	didn't it?

anyone	**everyone**	**no one**	**someone**

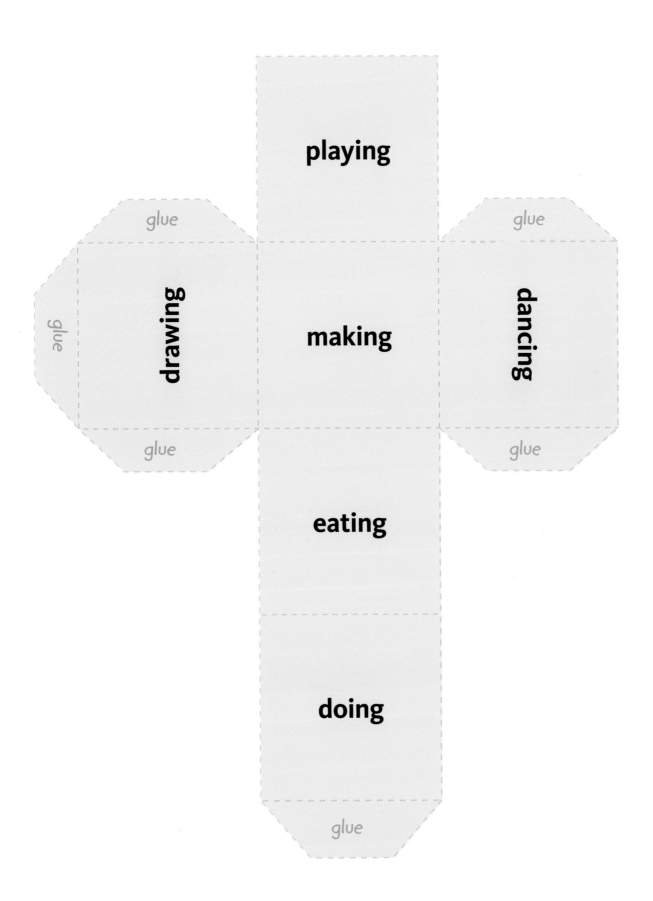

playing

glue

glue

drawing

glue

glue

making

dancing

glue

glue

eating

doing

glue

eruption	cold weather	steam	active volcano
hurricane	ash	lava	heat
rain	snow	sandstorm	tornado
flood	blizzard	heatwave	drought

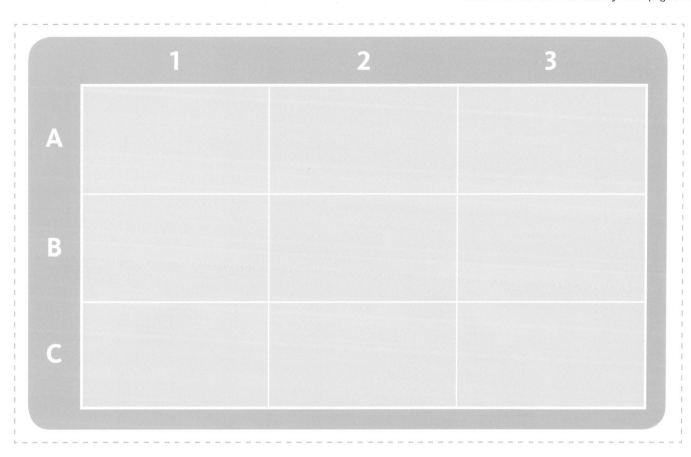

A water park

Horse riding

Whitewater rafting

Sightseeing

A photo safari

Camping

Playing tennis

Eating in a restaurant

Visiting a science or natural history museum

A visit to an aquarium

Walking on a mountain path

A beach